REMEMBER ME TO EVERYBODY

Frederick Gower Turnbull

Remember Me to Everybody

Letters from India, 1944 – 1949

EDITED BY BERNADETTE RULE

West Meadow Press

A T THE AGE OF TWENTY-THREE
Fred Turnbull, an English engineer, boarded an ocean liner
for India. It was 1944, the Second World War blazed on
every side, and Fred was leaving his native Yorkshire to
work at Jessop's Steel Company outside of Calcutta.
Jessop's was a large plant which produced one-fifth of the
steel for all of India, as well as designing and building
bridges, railway cars and other machines made from that
steel. In fact, it was Jessop's of Calcutta which rebuilt the
bridge over the River Kwai. Though he was intensely
excited at the prospect of working and living in such an
exotic place, Fred had no idea that he was arriving just in
time to witness the final years of the fabled British Raj, and
the birth of the independent nations of India and Pakistan.

Fortunately, Fred was a prolific letter-writer; even more
fortunately, he wrote well. His family saved every letter
that came, which was probably not even a quarter of those
he wrote home. Because of the tumultuous times, and
because of the vagaries of the postal service between India
and England, many of Fred's letters never arrived. Consequently, his first two years there are very scantily covered,

and much of his first impression is missing. But because of Fred's appetite for detail, his fascination for the way life unfolded around him never faded and, to the last, these letters enthusiastically record a world that is no more.

Whether he is describing the frantic social life of the British in their compound on the verge of the jungle, the jungle itself teeming with wildlife, its green blowing to silver in the teeth of a monsoon, or the Indians struggling to forge a new order out of a rich and chaotic mixture of cultures, religions and languages, Fred's is a voice we haven't heard before. Unlike earlier members of the British Raj, Fred did not come from the upper class. He was the eldest of three children of a steelworker and a homemaker who lived in the picturesque village of Ormesby at the foot of the moors. Ormesby itself was one of the last of the squireocracies in England, perhaps the last village to be lorded over by an active squire who took a patriarchal interest in the villagers. Fred's sister, Violet, remembers the squire and his wife sometimes stopping by the school to bid the children good morning. But when Fred feels homesick, it is not for some lost manor and servants, for steeplechasing and such. It is for a small house on a medieval abbey road, for a fence running beside two elms, a sycamore and a chestnut tree.

Fred always observes both his worlds with a clear, level gaze and high standards. Though he occasionally makes a comment which might seem racist towards Indians, or damning of the English, for the most part he is extremely compassionate towards everyone he observes so closely. He is of his time and place, unquestionably loyal to Britain; yet with his usual passionate idealism, he gradually becomes swept up in India's destiny as an independent nation as well. His understanding of Indian society, though necessarily limited, was enhanced by his gift for languages. Unlike the vast majority of Englishmen there, Fred became fluent in both Hindi and Bengali. This not only deepened his insight, but it also gained him an extra measure of respect from the men who worked under him at Jessop's.

For the most part Fred is addressing his mother in these letters, and a strong sense of unconditional love between them is evident from the tone. They are so frank and open that Fred himself may not have been completely aware of how much he reveals in them, but it is this honesty and his sense of humour which make them so compelling. They read like good fiction, giving Fred's personal story against the backdrop of political tension, with a well-drawn cast of secondary characters.

When Fred falls in love with an Anglo-Indian, the rules of his adopted society become even clearer. For an Englishman in his position to marry a "native" was strongly discouraged. Perhaps because of this, Fred introduces Ann to his mother a little at a time, referring to her first as one of a group of girls at a dance, then simply as "the bachelor of science." As a photographic image slowly appears in the developing bath, so Ann, and Fred's growing attachment to her, becomes clearer and clearer in the letters.

Despite the disapproval of Dum Dum society, Fred's characteristic stubborn idealism prevailed, and his love story is woven into the letters as it develops. However, it is the fact of Fred's tragic death which gives his letters their strongest resonance. Six months after his marriage, Fred was murdered in an anti British uprising at Jessop's. The story of his death, gleaned from firsthand accounts and newspaper reports, is the final testimony to his integrity.

On February 26, 1949, at about 10:30 in the morning,

the workers at the Jessop's plant moved away from their drills, lathes and cranes, and took up crowbars and shovels. Those who worked under Fred put him outside the factory gates and warned him to get to safety. However, as he was about to leave he looked back and saw his friend, Arthur Dwyer, being beaten and kicked by the mob.

"No!" he shouted, and ran back toward Dwyer, who by this time was being dragged, face-down, back into the factory. The mob quickly closed in on Fred as well and dragged him along. Both Dwyer and Fred were prodded with stoking irons into the factory furnace and burned alive. In another part of the plant, Fred Brennan was also killed in a pressure furnace, and a fourth man, Felix Augier, was stabbed to death.

The letters often foreshadow Fred's violent death as he describes the growing tensions around him. He laments the British government's exploitation of India. He writes with regret of the factory bosses' insensitivity towards the workers. Once, when telling of the murder of one of the compound's cooks, an old man whose friends ran away when he was attacked, Fred wonders how one could desert a friend at such a time. Indeed, when he was put to the ultimate test, he did not fail. With his courageous death, Fred Turnbull proved that he was as good as his word, and true to his ideals.

Yet death is not the subject of these letters. Life is Fred's subject, life in all its rich variety. The record they keep shows that he approached life the same way he finally approached death, at full tilt and wide open.

1944

Blythswood Hotel
Argyle Street
Glasgow
Monday [Feb.]

Dear Mam,

Just a couple of lines to let you know stage one of the journey is over. We actually bribed our way to Scotland. We had to change three times for Glasgow, with five minutes to catch each connection, in those five minutes we had to pile out of the carriage, rush into the luggage van, throw out our trunks, grab a hand barrow, stack them on it, and then trundle it perhaps two or three plat-forms away. Each time we had to cross the lines, we had to bribe a porter to take them over in the lift. With the shortage of staff, one has to see to one's own baggage. When we reached Glasgow (10 pm) we had to carry our bags a mile to the hotel. I tipped a Glasgow "razor slasher" to give us a hand.

This Hotel is terrific, there are 120 rooms on our floor, and we are on the 3rd floor. I had a bath this morning, tell Violet it is 100%.[1] I slunk through the corridor (is it slunk or slinked?) complete with dragon studded dressing gown, towel at the approved drape (a la I.C.I.).[2]

At present I don't know whether to learn Bengali or Glasgie Scotch.[3] Don't attempt to write me yet, I expect to embark today, so you will have to wait until I get a permanent address. Do you remember that book I required (Mechanical World Year Book)? I have just bought one round the corner for 2/6 and it is dated 1944. The trouble now is to get it past the censor (as long as he has some common censor we should manage it). This hotel life is just my handwriting, marvellous meals just when you want them, good service and a resident's lounge, with lager beer and a sprinkling of vacuous looking [lounge] lizards. They indulged in a little mild horse-play last night with us, trying to get us to accept some snuff. They are real tough guys, how they keep out of the army I don't know. Yet the army don't accept mental deficients, do they? Two glasses of Scotch ale and they begin to sing Nellie Dene. Drinking men. Baloney. I could drink more molten lead.

Well cheerio, and remember me to everybody, including pistol packin' Corporal Poppy Cooper.[4]

Love,
Fred

Wed. 8th March

This is the first chance I have had to send you a letter since boarding ship. The voyage up to now has been the laziest

time in my life. I will give you an example of a typical day
afloat. Bob Kraus and I share a cabin; at 7 am Abdul (that
is our Indian steward), wakes us, brings hot water, and
cleans our shoes. 7:45 am, the gong goes for breakfast,
which is a really good meal served in the dining hall. Here
again we have an Indian boy to serve two of us. After
breakfast I usually have a game or two of chess (there are
some good players on board). At 10 am I change my book
in the lounge library, and at 10:15 am I attend a
Hindustani class in the afterdeck smoke-room. 11 am I
have a mile walk, that is about 15 times round the ship on
the boat deck, then a game of darts, or deck quoits or
shuffleboard until lunch at noon. After lunch I sun-bathe
on deck, or read in the lounge. Usually we have a lot of
fun with a skipping rope. Tea is served at 3:30 pm after
which I usually have a hot bath in salt water (very invigo-
rating, but the soap won't lather). Dinner is ready for us at
6 pm and then each night is occupied in some game or
competition organized by the passengers' entertainments
committee. Brains Trust one night, a Quiz another night,
a whist drive, an evening of Housey-Housey[5] or sometimes a dance on deck. Every sport is organized and run as
a knock-out competition.

    The last session of the Brains Rust (as they call it)
included among its members, a doctor, an Archaeologist,
an Indian Barrister, the Consul-General of the Dutch East
Indies, an American lady journalist, and a tea-planter's
daughter, so you see, Joad & Co.[6] have nothing on us.
The passengers as you can see are very interesting. They
include Persian oil engineers, a great many British technicians, Ministry of Information and Consular employees,
businessmen, tea-planters and about a dozen nurses,
whose destination is China.

    I almost forgot to mention the bar we have on board,

where any drink can be obtained, and every brand of tobacco. Everything is sold duty-free, tobacco costs 6d[7] per oz., with cigarettes at 50 for 2/ = [8] with everything else in ratio.

I passed the customs without any trouble. There are a great many things I could have taken with me if I had known. I have not been seasick yet, except one day in mid-Atlantic there was a heavy swell and I felt a little light-headed, but now I have found my sea-legs and I find the roll of the ship quite pleasant. Last week we had a rough time in a rough sea. At mealtimes a frame is screwed round the table but the sugar still slides from one side to the other, the milk overturns or you find all the fish knives and the spoons piled on your plate, mixed up with your food. I had a bath that day, and first of all the water was up to my neck and next minute, I was left high and dry with my feet well submerged. I didn't know 9,000 tons of ship could perform like that.

Someday I hope you will have the thrill of a long sea voyage, Mam. Every three days I do an hour watch for U-boats. This is voluntary, but all of the passengers do it.

Remember me to as many of my friends as possible. then they won't feel badly if any of my letters go astray, or I forget to write to them. I am afraid you won't be able to reply to me for some time, but I will let you have my permanent address as soon as possible. Give my love to all at home. Violet would enjoy this life. Tell Arthur to travel if he ever gets the chance.

March

After 4 weeks away from home I am still at sea, the Red Sea to be exact. I don't know why it is called the Red Sea, probably because it is red hot. Night time is worst, and the cabins are intolerably stuffy, although we have electric fans going all night. There is no ventilation with the ship being blacked out; last night I slept(?) with only a pair of trunks on and one sheet over my legs, and when Abdul awoke me I was soaked in perspiration. The day-time dress is shirt and shorts. I bought this pair I am wearing now in Port Said, for 45 piastres. I have had to sew on all the buttons, and give the seams the 'once-over.' Otherwise they are a good pair. An Indian friend of mine from Leeds University showed me 'the ropes' or rather the threads, and I have made a good job of the sewing.

Well I have seen the sights since I left England, porpoises in the Atlantic, flying fish in the Red Sea, and sharks in the town of Port Said. I hope you received my Airgraph. I sent it from Simon Arzt large store. After tea we came ashore again, the Indian (Khan) and myself. We had a good time and finished up in a cabaret and dance, which we left in time to board the boat before twelve midnight. After leaving the show we had to pass through the native quarter to get back to the waterfront by midnight. The night was very dark, and there were only two of us (Khan and myself).

We didn't realize how dangerous our journey was, but luckily we reached the quayside without any trouble and were rowed across the harbour to our ship by one of the natives. Two men who followed us were beaten up, knocked out, and had their money stolen.

Port Said is certainly a rough place. The whole population seems to exist by peddling phoney goods, "You buy nice bracelet, Mister." Tommy Handley must have been here. The only word of Egyptian one needs to know is "Yallo," which is an impolite way of saying Buzz Off.

The view from the ship as it enters Port Said is wonderful. The road which runs alongside the harbour is fringed with palms and other tropical trees, and the hotels & stores which border the road are all built of white or yellow material, and the design is very impressive. From the waterfront stretch the main streets, full of large American cars tearing along on the right hand side, with a donkey cart plodding along among them now and then. The pedestrians are picturesquely garbed in a flowing white nightgown affair, with a tarbush for a head covering.

The water in the harbour is very clear and is dotted with small white rowing boats, each with its "gippy" oarsman. These fellows keep up a running flow of invective at each other in Arabic, & curse the police launches which tear dangerously past them, filled with colourfully dressed "gippy" police armed with rifles. Round the boat are floating Woolworth stores, selling everything from bananas to suitcases. They bob round the ship's side, & send up their wares in a basket on a rope which you pull up yourself. If they ask for £6 for an article, you offer them £1. Then they shout, "No no, Mr. McGregor" or "Mr. McKay." I bought forty oranges from them for 4/-,[9] Imagine this scene with a blue sky overhead and green water beneath. It is the most colourful sight I have ever seen, & we had a lot of fun, too, bartering with Mr. Harry Lauder in the nightshirt, & knocking his "fez" off with orange peel.

We left Port Said in the morning before I got up, &
then had a very interesting trip down the Suez Canal.
At Suez we picked up __[10] American Air Corps officers
& an Ensa party[11] all going to India. I made enquiries to
see if Boone Rose was with them, but he is not & Jean
McLaren is not with Ensa.

We had a laugh on board the other night at a session of
our Brains Trust. Two members were American officers,
& Ronald Frankaus' wife was included, too. One of the
questions asked was, "What is one of the most recent classics?" Well, everyone answered with his or her opinion, &
then came the turn of one of the Americans. His choice
was the book *Gone With The Wind*, & he waxed eloquent
about it. He described the characters, the authoress; he
went into detail about the American way of life it had
enshrined in our memories forever, & when he paused,
out of breath, a nasal voice at the back of the saloon said,
"I'll take it, miss."

Mention me to Mr. Cooper & the gang,[12] & give my
love to all at home. Tell Arthur & Violet I have not regret-
ted coming for one minute, & if they ever have the opportunity to travel they should certainly take it.

> Cheerio & love,
> Fred

c/o Jessop & Co. Ltd.
Rajahbagan
Dum Dum
Calcutta

14th June

Dear Mam,

I have just received an air-letter from you, also an airgraph; and a letter from Violet, another from Fred Barker at the 'Keys,'[13] and an air-graph from Ernie. That is how I am getting my mail, 'feast & famine,' nothing for 2 or 3 weeks, and then a bundle, all together.

The first rain of the Monsoon came this evening, a light shower (about 2 tons to the square inch in a minute) and was I glad, it smelt just like Corporation Road in January.[14] I pulled off my shirt & went up onto the roof, and let it beat down onto my bare back (the rain I mean). This is the first time I have heard of anyone going out into a downpour, and the rest of the day keeping out of the sun.

I am glad the invasion has started, it is a definite step toward ending the war. I feel I am missing something, not being in England at the present time. But then, we have our own little war here in Bengal. The Japs are still 40 miles inside Indian territory, so they are about as far from Dum Dum as London is from Ormesby, and they have no sea to cross to reach Calcutta.

Since we arrived in Dum Dum we have had the N.E.

Daily Gazette sent to us regularly from Middlesbrough
by Mrs. Kraus. I enjoy reading it too, 'specially little bits
like "Chicken-coop for sale, Gypsy Lane, Nunthorpe," or
to see what is on at the Odeon.

After the rain ceased tonight I went for a walk into the
jungle through the native villages. I wish I could get hold
of some film. I could take some marvellous snaps: bullock
carts, native dwellings, shrines & temples, palm trees, &
some of the customs of the natives. I could write a book
about them.

On the fringe of the jungle I came to a large lake (tanks,
as they are called in India. There is usually one every 100
yards when you leave the outskirts of any large town). On
the banks of this lake were a native and his small son (age
about four years) & they were fishing with a net, by the
simple means of wading in the water & pushing the net in
front of them. I asked them what they were catching, (my
Hindi is passable now), & the father explained that they
were catching shrimps. They ignored the fish, which were
soon covered with black ants as they ~~kicked~~ (fish don't
kick) wriggled on the bank.

I expect you are interested to know how I am fixed
financially. Well, income tax runs out at 47 chips (rupees)
a month, Provident fund 25 chips monthly, & house rent
10 chips every four weeks. In this is included water, rates
& electricity. I pay my bearer 20 chips, the cook buys &
cooks our food for 110 chips, the dhobi, or laundry, costs
me 9 chips, & bak-sheesh[15] to sweepers, gardeners, etc.
runs about 20 chips per month, so my actual cost of living
is about 250 chips a month (£18). This is a lot better than
I expected, 'specially the Income Tax, and at present I
have 800 chips to my credit in the National Bank of India,
so I should be able to buy the 'Keys' at the end of 5 years.

India is an interesting country, but I would not like to

spend all my life here. Already I have got the wanderlust again and when the Chung-King[16] plane roars over, I feel I would like to be moving on.

Strangely enough the Indian winter is almost perfect, climatically, April, May and June being the hottest months, followed by the Monsoon, when it rains without ceasing for days, sometimes weeks. Then comes holiday time, when most of the Europeans take their leave and go up to the hills, or down Madras way to Ootacamund where Mr. Howell is going for his leave. I don't know whether I shall be allowed a holiday this year, but around September & October there are many native festivals or Pujas as they are called; these religious holidays are all observed by the firm so I am sure of a few days' spell. During the Puja, the priests come into the works and paint gods on the machines and decorate the department. In fact, according to the 'old hands,' in peace-time everybody had a lot of fun, both masters & men, during these celebrations.

My work's bearer (I have 2, one in my office at work) today killed a snake outside the office, and although he said it was harmless, I didn't like the look of it.

Thank Violet for her letter. I will reply to them all when I find time. Remember me to all the gang, and tell Ernie I was very pleased to receive his and Fred Barker's letters. All the best to all at home, and write soon.

4 July

Thanks for your very interesting letter of May 10th with details of Ormesby activities. I would like to have gone to the dance in the 'Salute the Soldier' week. I have only been to two since I left home, one in Port Said & and one at the Cossipore Club on the first Sunday in June. Of course we often dance to a gramophone at parties or when out for dinner.[17] The gramophone, by the way, is indispensible in Dum-Dum, everyone has a 'pick-up'.[18]

My Hindi is getting better now. I can even make myself understood by these 'up-country' men. 'Pucca jungli wallas' they are too.[19]

There is talk of home-rule for India after the war, but I can't see it being a success. As an example I will tell you of one of my top marking men to illustrate the mentality of the average Indian. This man is an absolute wizard with drawings. He can't speak a word of English, yet he can read a blueprint written in English. He knows more about triangulation, theory of Pythagoras and practical setting out of levels than most English engineers, & yet he won't tell me his wife's name because it is against his caste laws, & if a machine persistently breaks down, he seriously suggests having a 'Puja' on it. A 'Puja' is a religious holiday or festival, when the native priests enter the works, anoint all the machines, paint Indian gods all over the place, and decorate cranes and structures with garlands of flowers.

In September there are several of these Pujas. On these days the whole Structural works are given over to the priests for carrying out all their religious ceremonies.

During this time the Sahibs are their guests, native food, & native brewed palm tree alcohol is in abundance, and the men are insulted if the Sahibs don't 'polish off' all that is set before them.

The Indian is certainly a complex fellow. He has a keen natural intelligence, but centuries of the caste system has left its mark, & at times he is very childlike. Many times at work I have a job to keep my face straight when I see anything humourous. The other day a driller came to me. He is 54 years old, 4 feet, 6 inches tall, he has ten children, and honestly I would take him to be 12 years old if he hadn't a long black beard. The bottom of the said black beard has been dyed red because he has made the Pilgrimage to Mecca. He said he was very sick, because he had eaten too many mangoes, and if I permitted him to go home, he would pray for me, because I was the 'father of the poor.'

You should see the letters I receive from them requesting a rise in wages. Naturally none of them can speak or write English so they pay an anna and get a second rate 'babu' (native clerk) to draw up the letter for them. The letter usually begins like this: "Respected & honoured sir, I most humbly beg to lay the following facts of my grievance before your esteemed perusal. I am supporting 10 members of my family, which is impossible." The letter then carries on in the same vein (the writing and spelling atrocious) and ends up promising to be my lifelong servant & that he will offer up prayers for my future happiness. I have actually seen a letter requesting a month's leave to go up-country for his "grate & osspicious marriage to a lady" & this letter ended with: "If you grant my request I will pray to you, as you pray to your patron saint J. Christ Esq."

The pay of the workmen is about 10 annas a day for

coolies, rising to craftsmen at 2 rupees a day. When I first came out here I thought this scale of pay was worse than criminal, but now I realize these fellows save at least half of it. Suppose that I granted the workmen's request for an increment, they then work for a month & then clear off up-country for 3 months to live on the extra money. Or sometimes, if they get an increase in pay, they take one extra day a week off. They are a happy-go-lucky lot. They live on one good meal of rice a day, with perhaps a coco-nut or a couple of mangoes they can scrounge. Possibly ten of them will build a bamboo shack in the jungle behind the works so their rent costs them nothing. After working for a year or two they have enough money saved to retire, or set themselves up in a business as cobbler or hairdresser or rickshaw-boy.

The clothes I left England with I have never worn, except the undershirts, which I wear when it is extremely hot, to absorb the perspiration. I now own about 25 shirts, 12 pairs of shorts, 10 pairs of long white trousers, and the tailor is still working making me 3 light suits. The sticky climate here means changing one's clothes at least twice a day if one wants to feel clean.

Every tradesman comes up to the house. Every week we have the washerman, every two weeks the barber, the tailor comes at least once a week, the babu who is giving us Hindi lessons arrives every Monday & Friday. We pay everybody monthly so on the first of the month we settle up and you can imagine the crowd which files into my room. In addition to the tradesmen, I have my own bearer, cook, sweeper and gardener to pay. The total amount is usually in the region of 250 chips (work that out at 1/6 per chip).[20]

Well Mam, I have got writer's cramp so I hope every-one at home is fit. Remember me to the gang, and if you

hear of anyone I know expecting to call at Calcutta, let
them have my address, I will be pleased to meet anyone
from home. So cheerio & all the best

August 4th

Just received two of your air-mail letters. I think you had
better send your future letters by ordinary mail, air-mail is
too expensive & really there is not much difference in the
time between air and ordinary mail.

The monsoon is still doing its best to flood us out. It
has rained every day for 5 weeks, & the nights are warm
and sticky. All the sahibs & most of the native population
carry umbrellas. When I first saw them I said, "Never
will I sink so low as to carry one of those things. Why in
England, only parsons and women use them." Incidentally, now I always carry one. If one wore a raincoat
(even during raining it is still hot), one becomes so
soaked with perspiration that it is a waste of time, so you
can see the advantage of an umbrella.

Of course there are sunny spells between showers, and
I have seen some interesting wildlife (including Jungli
wallas). The previous week we had a day holiday, it was
some Hindu festival, & I decided to have a morning in
bed. From my window I can see the front lawn and
further away the edge of the jungle. I was watching the
parrots dropping down out of the palms & feeding on
sunflower seeds. On the other side of the compound
stands a gaunt skeleton of a tree without a leaf on it,
anywhere. When I went to the window, the parrots all

flew onto this tree. I don't know whether you can imagine this sight, but the tree seemed as green and bushy and
leafy as all other trees, but every leaf was a parrot. It was
marvellous.

Just the other day, as I came home for 'tiffin,'[21] I
noticed the adjacent field black with vultures. A
water-buffalo had died and a couple of Mahommedans
(Hindus never eat beef, the cow is holy to them) were
cutting off some choice steaks. The vultures were patient-
ly waiting for the carcass. There were thousands of them,
big, ungainly birds, each about 3 feet high. A pack of
pariah dogs from the nearby native village were chasing
round snapping at the birds. As the dogs came within
striking distance, each vulture made an ungraceful jump
into the air and landed again behind the dogs. It was a
sort of leap-frog & everyone seemed to enjoy it.

Last week I had the privilege of witnessing a native
judicial rite, & was I interested! One of the men in the
blacksmith's shop had been robbed of 380 chips, so the
workmen formed their own council of justice. The
suspects, 12 in number, were made to sit round in a circle
& put a handful of rice in their mouths. After a stipulated
time had elapsed each man had to spit out his mouthful of
rice onto the floor. The jury then inspected it, & if it was
moist the man was absolved from suspicion. Sure
enough, one man's rice was dry, and he broke down &
confessed, so the council turned him over to the police.

This way of catching a thief, although crude, is logical
and efficient. Evidently the man who is guilty is so scared
the flow of saliva in his mouth is restricted, & consequently he spits out his rice dry. The men tell me this
method has never been known to fail.

There is also another method used up-country. After
any crime has been committed, the suspects are rounded

up & each one is given a small stick or a match-stalk. The suspects are then told to return in a week & compare the length of the sticks, as the stick belonging to the guilty man will grow longer than the others. Practically every-time, the guilty man breaks a piece off his matchstick because he is scared it will grow bigger. So when they compare sticks finally, the man owning the shortest stick is the guilty man.

Well Mam, that is enough of primitive justice. I thought of you all on Bank Holiday Monday. I expect you are all preparing for your holidays. Incidentally, I will be off this Friday. It is a Hindu Puja, "Janmastami," a feast to one of their gods. I wish they had a few more gods, then I should get a few more holidays.

The last two weeks I have seen two good films in Calcutta, "For Whom the Bell Tolls" and "Northern Pursuit," also a film called "Jane Eyre," a typical Orson Welles' production, it seemed more of a comedy to me than a serious film.

I was surprised to hear Albert & Tommy Elliott were both in India.[22] If you ever hear of anyone passing through Calcutta, let them know my address. I would be pleased to see any of the old gang. The other day I saw an old issue of the 'gazette.' I was rather amused to read that around the straits of Dover was sweltering in a heat wave, the temperature being between 70° & 80°. After a shower of rain here the other night the temperature fell to 85° & I felt almost frozen.

This news may be of interest to Dad. In the works we are well through production of the second floating dock that Jessops have made. These docks are exactly the same pattern as the one the Japs captured at Singapore. These docks, as you probably know, are the largest in the world, being big enough to accommodate the Queen Mary. I feel

a personal pride in this last one, having personally super-
vised all marking and drilling on it, this being my first job
at Jessops.

Well, I hope you are all fit at home & hope you all have
a good time when the war is over.

Aug. 15th

I received 2 letters from you 3 weeks ago & have just had a
newsy epistle from Ernie. He says he received a letter &
an airgraph within 2 days. This must mean that they take
about the same time to England, but coming out here
there is a difference of 4 to 5 weeks between time taken by
letters & airgraphs.

Last Friday I had a day holiday, "Janmastami." It is a
feast to the Hindu god Krishna. Most of the workmen
attended the works on Saturday wearing bracelettes of
tinsel and ribbon. It is an old custom of the days of Indian
Chivalry (long since gone) when besieged princesses
sent their bangles to the Moghuls. The Moghuls were
compelled by tradition to rescue the princesses, but were
never allowed to see them. Well anyway, on Friday I
didn't rescue any Indian Princesses, I just spent the day in
Calcutta, incidentally spending about 100 chips (£ 7-10 to
you foreigners) on clothes.

I don't know whether I have ever told you but out
here all laundry is done by the dhobi (washerman). The
traditional method of washing clothes has remained
unchanged for centuries. The water (provided by nature)
being a small lake (tanks we call them and Dum Dum has

thousands). The clothes are soaked in water and then
flayed onto the dhobi stone. These stones are hollowed in
the middle, worn by the dhobi of each decade flaying the
laundry on them. Well, you can imagine the state clothes
become after a few cleanings. Countless white women
have lost their reason through this practice. Last week I
had a pair of shorts returned looking like a Hawaiian grass
skirt & my shirts resemble 'Shredded Wheat.' All drying is
done by pegging the clothes out in the sun, so with the
coming of the rains we can't get our laundry returned.
That is why I am buying so many new clothes.

Just a little word in favour of dhobis: provided he is an
expert, a pair of white trousers can be made really perfect.
I think the sun bleaches the cloth, and when properly
washed and pressed they look immaculate.

Just as a point of interest, since I arrived in India I have
had breakfast in bed every single morning.

Ernie was interested in whether we are rationed in
Bengal. We certainly are, but it is a triumph of muddle &
graft. We are in the unusual position of being rationed
one side of the road & unrationed the other. Parts of India
have no food control whatever.

At the works they all receive their rations through
Jessop's own food office, and about 6 weeks ago they
all complained about the quality of the rice & threatened
to strike. Things looked pretty bad for a time, & then
eventually the whole 3 works, Mechanical, Structural &
Wagon Works, employees totalling over 10,000 Indians,
refused to take their rations of rice, salt, mustard oil,
lentils & wheat flour, for 3 weeks. When one realizes that
these men also draw rations for their families, quite an
amount of food is involved. This refusal to accept their
rations proves that they were getting fed somewhere, &
to my knowledge, nobody starved.

I, too, am rationed through Jessops, & during this
trouble, the workmen had a picket of jungli wallas outside
the ration office to see no one twisted & drew his rations.
My bearer was scared to go for my rations because
another bearer, from across the compound, had been
beaten up by these jungli fellows when he went for his
sahib's rations.

India is no place to live, Mam. Everyone here lives
either in luxury or abject poverty, & disease is everywhere.
Every man in my shop has malignant malaria & period-
ically it strikes them down. Everyday I sign 2 or 3 sick
notes. They (the men) come to me, burning eyes, terrific
temperature & their bodies shaking with fever, & ask for a
week's leave, after which they return to work with their
bodies burnt away with the fever. They also lose much
time with cuts and bad feet.

If this country is handed over to the Indians it will be
the worst step possible. The high caste Indians treat the
lower castes much worse than the white man does.

India is a country which goes to extremes in everything. It is a jumble of modern progress & backward
custom. Just imagine in these times of modern rationing
of foodstuffs, the images of the gods in the temples
receive their allowance of food, so the people can sacrifice
to them.

A young Brahmin clerk in my office was married today.
He invited me to the wedding feast at his home in
Shamnagar, but unfortunately I couldn't get the car, and
as Shamnagar is over 20 miles from here, I couldn't
attend. To recompense me for missing the feast, tonight
he sent me an earthenware bowl filled with Indian sweets
& delicacies, which I promptly handed to the gardener,
after nibbling a "Sunedash," a sweet made from the curds
of buffalo milk.

But I meant to tell you of this 26 year old Brahmin. His father many years ago lived in Madras, & there he became friendly with another Brahmin, & they decided as one had a son & one a daughter, to marry them off. Kanai, my young clerk, will see his wife today for the first time. This boy is wonderful at calculations, & his memory is phenomenal; it beats me how anyone so intelligent could put up with this system, but he says it is the Hindu law.

I have another marking boy, also 26 years of age & a middle caste Hindu. His name is Munghal & he is not very bright, but is a pleasant lad. The other day I jokingly asked him when he was going to get married, and he replied, "I have been married 4 years & my wife is now 10 years old," so he married her when she was 6 years of age. When he becomes a top Mistri[23] his father-in-law has told him she can come & live with him. So I told him not to worry, the way he's shaping now, she will never come to live with him. The same lad came to me the other day really scared because his brass identity disc had been stamped with M for Mohammedan instead of H for Hindu.

One of my Muslim platers came back from leave this week. His name is Hussein Ali & he took seven weeks instead of the month I allowed him. He went to his village, up in eastern Bengal somewhere, & the reason he was three weeks overdue, was that when he reached his village (by boat, everything is submerged in the floods caused by the monsoon), he couldn't find it. All the houses were under water, so he had to search three weeks in the jungle to find his wife.

Well, Mam, I intend to save as much money as I can here & then travel again. I have met people who have lived & moved about in almost every country in the world, & there seems to be no doubt about it, everyone is

unanimously agreed that New Zealand is the finest country in the world. India, & especially Burma, are the places
to make money, and then the general idea is to retire in
New Zealand. I am just realising that I am a young man &
that I have not seen half the world yet. So after the war I
may go into Burma when Jessop's open up their interests
there again.

Best of luck for now, Mam, & have a good time as soon
as the war is over. Give my love to the H.G. roughs & all
at home.

15 October

Sunday evening & I have an hour to spare to write to you.
I am going out to dinner tonight, with a game of poker
afterward very popular here. Poker has taken the place of
bridge. The weather is getting cooler now, in fact, early in
the morning the slight mist reminds me of June or July in
England. I often think of Ormesby, the sun on the hills
above the trees on Normanby road, the same trees I used
to climb a few years back. If I remember correctly, as one
turns the corner toward Huddlestones' farm the first tree
on the right is an elm, then another elm, a sycamore & a
chestnut. The picture of the chestnut is very clear. If I
stood on the top railing, I could just reach a small broken
off branch above me, and after getting my leg over that,
the conkers were mine.[24]

Tell me about Ormesby when you write, Mam. I
expect hay time is well over now & harvest time; when I
went for the first interview for this job to London, I

remember the stooks of corn in all the fields as I looked out of the train window. That is over a year ago. Time certainly flies and much has happened since then. Early next month (November) I am to be initiated in the 'Freemasons.' I wonder what Dad thinks of this.

Yesterday I paid 280 chips for a dress suit. That is £21 in your money. I suppose that is a lot for an evening dress, but I can go anywhere with it & know that I can "pass muster" with the best dressed people. I think it pays to buy a really good suit, & the cut of this one is 100% perfect. You know how particular I am about clothes. Unfortunately, clothes make the man in this world, especially the Indian world.

After a three week spell without any mail, I received three letters from you, & one from E.C. Ernie tells me he called on Aunt Liz in Rotherham. I bet she was surprised.

By the way, Mam, if you have any decent photographs of the family that you can spare, please let me have them. All my other photographs were stolen, including my birth certificate. A lot of Indians will steal anything. They will stoop to any means to swindle or extract another anna from one.

Last night in the Club I was speaking to some friends of mine (a Mr. & Mrs. Barclay) & the subject was politics. I happened to mention C.E. Joad representing Middlesbro'. Six R.A.F. sergeants were playing snooker in the same room & one came over & said, "Excuse me, but did I hear someone mention Middlesbro'?" After kissing each other on both cheeks, we found that he lives in Stockton & also his pal. We spent the evening reminiscing & travelling from High St., Stockton, across the "wilderness" to Middlesbro. His name is Harry Mallaby and he has invited us over to their sergeant's mess.[25]

I expect you think that all my time is spent socially,

larking round in cars, etc., but believe me I am certainly working hard. I have had to use my brains more than ever before. Tell Dad that the steelwork of Jessop's floating dock has been completed. This is the second, the first is in commission. These docks, being the largest in the world, can lift the 'Queen Mary.' The total output of structural steel in the whole of India is 10,000 tons per month, & of this total Jessop's make 2,000 tons a month, so you have some idea of the size of our works.

Well, Mam, keep your health & have a good time. All the very best wishes to you all.

Love,
Fred

1945

12 January

Dear Mam,

Have just received your parcel containing the I.L. News,[26] thanks a lot. I appreciate any good reading matter. I am sending a couple of snaps. Although the camera shutter was out of order & war-time printing paper is not so hot, they convey a picture of myself which I could never do in writing. No. 1 snap, with myself as the brutal overseer; that is the veranda of my house behind me. I am wearing mosquito boots, & you can get a rough idea of the colour of my face, if you compare it with my white shirt. I don't always look like this, but I have got my pipe in my mouth, and am expecting a fall of soot or something. Snap No. 2 is of myself & the London fellow. That is actually hair on his chest & shoulders, & I seem to have grown a beard, which is a photographic error. The conversation at this juncture was running as follows: Pete (London fellow), "Go on, put your feet in, like me, & watch the dicky bird."

Yorkshireman (ex Colonel, Home Guard), "No! I shall sit sideways in the sun, so that the photograph does full

justice to my powerful shoulders." After which, some
dirty so and so pushed me in the 'pani,' (Hindi for Adam's
Ale).[27]

Remember, Mam, I would like some snaps of you-all,
if you can spare any.

In my last letter I told you that I intended putting in
for a raise. I am doing ten mens' work here (nine of them
are cripples) & I was not saving enough money in my
opinion after paying for the necessities of life in India.
Well anyway, I saw the directors & they agreed that I
should be putting a little bit in the bank for a rainy day (or
for when I get married. Same thing), so I should get an
increase after the next board meeting. Tell Arthur that
when he wants anything in this world, just ask for it,
unless it is unreasonable.

I hope Teeside is not too cold now. I remember those
January Nor'easters (brrrr) and feel sorry for you-all. We
here in Calcutta have just experienced a cold snap, one
night the temperature fell to 45. Personally I enjoy it and
find it quite bracing.

Good luck and best wishes to all at home & keep in
good health. By the way, next Sunday I have been invited
to a wild pig shoot up country. I hope I can make it, but
we are extremely busy at present. Anyway, if it comes off I
shall let you know. Don't forget to write, & cheerio.

20 September

I am writing this full-size letter for 3 reasons: first, I have
nothing else to do tonight, secondly, I have had 6 letters

in 6 days from you, so I have to catch up on a little 'back' mail, and thirdly, while air-letters are very handy, they are rather limited in space & so often, when I am in the middle of telling some tale, I find I have come to the end of the last page & so, have to dry up in a hurry, so to speak.

We had a letter from Harry[28] & although it was strictly censored, I understand that he had had 3 weeks holiday in either the south of India, or Ceylon. He also mentioned that his 'tour is over' as they say in the R.A.F. & he expects to be home before Christmas. Another thing that he mentioned which made me green with envy was the fact that he is saving 400 rupees per month & he had just received 2800 rupees, back pay, which is more than I have saved since I have been in India. During the fighting in the Mediterranean, Harry was flying in torpedo-bombers round Malta, so I suppose he has earned his easy time in India. He admits that it is a "money for jam" job that he is in now. He doesn't even work after tiffin, & the money he has saved will really start him off well in "civvy street."

Just at present Calcutta transport is in a state of chaos. All the tramways employees are on strike & as Calcutta has a population of about 4 million & most of them travel by tram to & from work, you can imagine the confusion, because the bus service is inadequate and old fashioned. There is some talk too of the rickshaw wallahs, taxi drivers & gharry wallahs going on strike in sympathy, & then there will be some fun.

Sept. 24th

Since I commenced this letter & boasted about the number of letters I had received up to the 20th, I haven't had another one from any source, which is unusual, and the lads are worse than me, they haven't had any mail for a

week now. By the way, Pete got your letter and thanks you
for it. He is almost fit again and has finished his course of
injections for dysentery.

Last Sunday Pete & I went to Calcutta Swimming
Club once more for the day. Bob couldn't come. He had a
peculiar ailment which is known as 'Spider's lick.' This one
is a pip, I will have to describe it in detail. It is the 5th time
Bob has contracted it, but so far Pete and I have been
lucky. First of all, it is not caused by a spider, but by a
small insect which either lays eggs under one's skin, drops
saliva onto the skin, or worse. Anyway, not even doctors
know what sort of operation this insect performs, but the
infected part becomes sore, inflamed and then breaks,
after which it spreads to about the size of a half crown.
Then one can scald, burn, apply lotion, liniment, cream,
salve, oil or powder to the seat of the trouble, but it has
no effect, & dries up and disappears in its own time,
usually about 2 weeks. Bob has got two licks or bites
(whatever you wish to call them) on the end of his nose &
on his lip.

Just a couple of weeks ago I lost a couple of nights'
sleep through ear-ache & went to the works' doctor to
have them syringed & oiled. The doctor blamed the
swimming, but eventually found out the real cause of the
trouble, another insect. This friendly little beetle enters
the ear & lives there until rooted out. Marvellous place,
Bengal, isn't it? I think between the three of us, we have
had every tropical disease known (& unknown) to man.
But then it is all in the game & we get plenty of laughs
from each others' troubles & moans.

Of course India has its good points & compensations.
Take the Swimming Club, for instance. I often wish that
you and Violet could spend a day there with me. A canvas
chair & cane table under a large canopy; breakfast, tiffin &
dinner served when required; everybody lounging about

in brief costumes; the wide view of the pool, with the cool green water; a hot sun with a stretch of grass for sunbathing; a game of water-polo in progress in the deep end and all the European kids of Calcutta in the shallow; a bronzed gang of young folk, splashing and pushing each other off the big raft in the centre, and always a crowd of Americans wise-cracking in the middle.

Our programme usually starts off with a big breakfast, followed by a cigarette & a talk until the meal has settled, & then half an hour's swimming while the water is still cool. Then we sprawl about in the sun, sleep, sunbathe, talk, swim, eat, until it is time to get changed & get back into Calcutta for a picture show. Sounds good, doesn't it?

Last Sunday we were sitting just behind a French girl & boy who were standing on the water's edge pattering away in their own language & evidently deciding to swim under water to the far side (they were both in swimming costumes). Presently they were joined by 2 young French officers of the French Air Force, & these fellows wore khaki shorts & shirts and evidently couldn't find costumes. After being introduced all round, the officers decided to throw the girl into the water, so the 3 men each grabbed a leg or an arm, shouted 1,2,3 in French and heaved the girl up above the water. Anyway, something went wrong & one of the officers forgot to leave go, for the next minute he hit the water with a terrific splash & when he dragged himself out, like a drowned rat, he pattered away in French quicker than I can speak Hindi. It was really very amusing.

Just after tea it started to rain & by 8pm it was tanking with a real storm raging. Pete and I got a taxi to the pictures and while we were in the cinema we could hear the rain drumming on the roof. After the show we waited outside because we had fixed up for the works' car, a big station wagon, to pick us up.

Eventually it arrived, half an hour late, and the driver blamed floods on the road into town. Coming back we had to make a wide detour to miss the flooded roads & looking out of the side windows reminded me of travelling in a speed-boat, with the clouds of spray shooting out from under the front wheels. The ride along the deserted road after we left behind the suburbs of Calcutta was grand, a cool breeze blowing and a bright moon lighting up the swamps and jungle.

Today, after an extremely hot morning, the sky clouded over at tiffin time, and we had just finished our meal when the thunder started & after a few minutes of blinding flashes & ear-splitting bangs, a pucca tornado hit us. Windows banged, everything in the house which could fall down did so, & outside, branches of trees were falling and bashing their way earthwards whichever direction we looked in. After it eased up, the compound was completely under water, with leaves and branches floating on the surface. This should be the last of the monsoon, with the prospect of 6 months of perfect weather ahead of us.

Well, Mam, time I dried up & climbed into bed because I have a busy week ahead of me, cleaning up my department before I go on leave. Best wishes to all at home & those in the navy. I intend to write to Arthur soon. He said send my letters to you because he didn't know where he would be posted in the next few days. I still haven't found the opportunity to buy Diana Vincent anything yet, but am still trying.[29]

Cheerio & love
Fred

1946

Feb. 3rd

Dear Violet,

First I will say how disappointed I am that so far it has
been impossible to send the shoes. I had hoped to get
them to Avonholme by your birthday, but so far there has
been much letter writing with lashings of red tape & a
dash of Bureaucracy. At present there is a sort of triangu-
lar duel between the "Export Trade Controller, Calcutta"
the "Department of Supply, New Delhi," and the
"Department of Food, New Delhi,"[30] with myself as the
party of the first part. The point or bone of centention is
whether shoes constitute: (a) an article of export, (b) an
article of supply, or (c) an article of food. Personally I
don't think that the Dept. of Food have a leg to stand on.
Unfortunately, all my old service friends have left this
land of milk & honey, so I can no longer send parcels
through courtesy of the R.A.F.
    The following statement may not seem relevant to the
haggling over sending parcels, but, this particular slice of
the British Empire (India is a big slice, too) on which the
sun never sets, is definitely lost to Britain, & does not

even remain friendly to her former mistress (that looks
bad, substitute Master) & the reason for this state of
affairs is the bungling, the dithering, of the pompous,
chair-borne, old-school-tie, buck-passing, stuffed-shirt
breed that our Public Schools churn out. The very same
idiots who slip & slide through an immoral life in a
whiskey-sodden stupor, tangle industry, commerce &
Government dealings with red tape & letters in triplicate,
hold down the highest paid jobs without doing a day's
work, think in terms of race and class distinction, & are to
be found at the top of all Government Depts., the Indian
Army & all Government controlled firms and projects.

If necessary to stamp out this type, I would even join
the bourgeois or proletariat or whatever it is called & join
you in drinking vodka & wearing a red tie (no,no, anything
but the red tie). Well anyway, I shall wear a red nose.[31]

Within 2 years, India will get her Swaraj, her independence & after pushing out the sahibs, will drift away
entirely from Britain, while her students can shout 'Jai
Hind'[32] until their lungs burst. This severance from the
Empire will be a bad knock for Britain & a worse deal for
India. This country definitely is not, & won't be for many
more years, in a position to govern herself. Graft and
bribery is too rife, the masses are too castebound & uneducated to understand or take part in home rule, and there
are too many rival factions to make a peaceable understanding possible. With sensible handling in the last
decade, this situation would never have arisen, & with the
developing of this country's Industrial potential, both
England and India would have benefitted tremendously.
Now the Labour Government are left 'holding the baby,'
and have the difficult task of sorting out this problem
with the prospect of much criticism from the Tory Party,
the people who are responsible.

Feb. 7th

Today received an air-letter from Mam, this is the 2nd in 2
weeks. Something has definitely gone wrong with the
England-India postal service. It is rather amusing. Pete,
Bob & myself have each had a letter starting "Nice to hear
from you once more," or "Hope you are alright," or
(mine) "Good to hear from you after such a long time."
The Calcutta postmen have given notice of a strike, but I
don't know whether this is responsible for loss of mail.

Yesterday was Saraswati Puja (or Sripanchami), the
Goddess of learning, but all we learnt was that it was a
holiday, so we spent the day at Jessops' Club, swimming
and lying on our backs, watching vultures & kite-hawks
wheel in the cloudless sky. By the way, the snaps I have
enclosed are all taken round the new Swimming Pool.
The one of Bob is rather blurred, but gives some idea of
the background of trees behind the pool, palms & cotton-
trees. Incidentally, the small twisted palm at the right, at
the back is the result of the natives cutting gashes in the
trunk from which they collect the sap to make palm
toddy. I have never tasted this drink, but know it is very
potent, like the Mexican tequila. The pool, diving stand,
railings, steps were all made from scrap in the structural
works.

The snaps have come out remarkably well. They were
all action snaps and were taken just before we actually
dived. Jim Bell is the latest acquisition to Jessop & Co.
A Scot and a most profound & comical fellow, everything
he does is the signal for roars of laughter. He has a mourn-
ful face & a zest for living & a sense of humour which
belie his looks. The other snap includes Nicky, our faith-
ful tripehound, & even if his pedigree is doubtful, he is a
really intelligent dog and a likeable little animal too.

Well, Violet, the mosquitoes are eating me alive, so I

dry up, after wishing you astonishing luck & good wishes
for your birthday.

Mar. 19th

Dear Mam,

Quite a long time since I wrote a 'pucca' letter so here we
go, & anyway this one at least should get through, having
paid - /14/-[33] for it & will help to clear up one or two
things I am doubtful about. First, did Vince write me a
letter lately? I received one written on 11/12/45 but none
since. Also, do you know if Mrs. Layfield[34] received her
letter from me? Also, have you received January's cheque
yet & are any more missing? If you keep me informed I
can fix things up from this end.

   Now, I have mentioned this before, but the letter may
be lost. Starting from Mar. 15th, I have told my Bank to
send you 250 rupees a month & they have already sent the
first cheque. Things are moving so quickly in India at
present (I mean politically) that Independence may come
to the Indians sooner than expected. Anyway, I don't
want to get what little money I have saved tied up in this
country or frozen in any international jiggery pokery in
the exchange, or find that the Rupee has been devalued
overnight to 2∂ a dozen. I was set on buying a car within
the next 3 months, but if I did the 'Goondahs' would
probably bum it during the next riots,[35] so the obvious
thing to do is to transfer what I can to England. You still
keep your pocket money out of it, & please put the rest

into the bank for me. Of course I don't mind if you take
the lot if you are hard up at any time. There is just another
point, Mam, Dad will know about it anyway. If the
money goes into National Savings Certificates there is a
limit to the amount which can be invested in any one
issue & I already have quite a few certificates with you.

I see in the papers that England has had the coldest
March for 35 years, & we in Bengal have had the hottest
March for about the same period, & mosquitoes, billions
of them. Even now they are biting hell out of my legs
under the table, even though I spray Flit (insect killer) at
15 minute intervals. But I think they thrive on the stuff (&
thrive on me too). The other night I slept with my arm
touching the net & in the morning I called in to see the
Works' Doctor to get some ointment applied to ease the
pain & the swelling. The Doc is a Bengali, Bishnu by
name, & in his quaint way he said, "Yas Mr. Tremble, I am
thinking you are too healthy. Your blood is very sweet-
ness, the mosquitoes are attracting for you," (& he sure
spoke a mouthful).

Again about the loss of mail, I had a letter from Mrs.
Cooper saying it was ages since they heard from me, &
also one from Maurice Jamieson from which I gathered
that he didn't get one of mine & I didn't get one of his.
Also I have written to May Garnham without a reply, so
she either didn't receive it, or else she has gone back to
England on de-mob.

Going through your old mail just now I found one
written on Jan. 25th mentioning that Violet knew a lady
whose daughter knew a fellow who knew he would have
to walk home if he didn't borrow a bike. Well I have been
thinking it over & can remember 5 girls from whom I
borrowed a bike after missing the last bus. Three of the

girls never knew that I was going to India, & of the other
2, one girl was named (I think it was Evelyn) Frost & the
other girl was named Margery (Something) & she lived in
or around Orwell Street. I didn't do so badly those days,
but now I don't know what a girl looks like.

As I said before, the weather is terrific, hot & sticky
intervals of sweating with periods of perspiration. So we
spend all our available spare time in the Swimming Pool,
weekends, evenings after work & even to 10 & 11 o'clock
at night.

March 21st

Since I started this letter, Mr. Doak (the Mechanical
Works' and Pete's manager) has left for England, Jimmy
Bell has got appendicitis & is in hospital, and Mr. & Mrs.
Duke have moved from Calcutta to occupy Mr. Doak's
bungalow in our compound. There are so many of
Jessops' people going on leave that they can't find any-
body to fill the vacant bungalows. Consequently there is
no hurry to move us into No. 10 Post Office Road.

One of the Mechanical foremen, Mr. Blakely, who is a
West Indian (Jamaica or someplace) has just come back
from doing a job in Burnpur near Asansol. He met
Norman Chester, who has just recovered from enteric
fever he says. Also he met a few more Middlesbrough
lads, Johnny & Jimmy Brennan, Ernie Jones, & a lad
named Docherty. Most of them worked at Cargo Fleet[36]
at some time.

Tonight I am writing to the New Zealand office in
Calcutta to see if they have any details or literature on
immigration into that country. I would still like to go
there to live.

I am enclosing the Second of exchange of the lost

January cheque in this letter, so if you have not received the first, cash this one in the usual manner. But if you have had the Jan. cheque by the time you receive this, destroy this one enclosed & use the first of exchange.[37]

On Saturday morning I go to record my vote, or rather 4 votes; as all the candidates are Bengalis, it doesn't matter who gets in, it is all a wangle. But I am enclosing a card with the names of 4 Babus who have just been in to see me & to do a little canvassing. (Babus is a courtesy title, like the English Mr.)

Well Mam, I hope you all keep fit & get plenty to eat. We don't starve here, though there's not much variety, but still we keep 100% fit. Best of luck to you all, including that peril of the deep, Admiral Turnbull.

[Names on enclosed card: Dr. Amar Kumar Das
Mr. Gonesh Lal Sonar
Mr. Kartic Chandra Shaw
Mr. Sushil Kumar Guha]

May 29th

I started this letter because I found that, after completing one air letter to you tonight, I had left a lot of things unsaid (or unwritten).

Peter leaves for Bombay by train on Friday, 31st May, so once more I shall have to say goodbye (for the present) to another friend, & although Shakespeare said, "Parting is such sweet sorrow," well, personally I think it is pretty lousy. I am afraid I will never get very tough in this line.

Lately he has spent very little time in the works, but has been out at "Cooks" or Head Office or just shopping. Today he was out with Joan Farren getting some more things for his wife. He brought home some silk under-wear so sheer that it can be passed through a wedding ring.

I will miss old Pete, not because he hasn't any faults, but because he is a damned likeable chap & we "get on together." I remember about 12 months ago he was extremely hard up, so I lent him 300 chips to buy a suit, & later 500 chips when we were on leave together when he was "broke." He appreciated the loan but, being spoilt as a child, he didn't rush to pay it back for four or five months. Finally I got fed up, knowing that he was sending 250 chips home to his wife per month. So one day I pinned him down & told him that he & I both drew the same wages & I didn't see why I should keep his wife & son out of my money, & that, if he thought anything about play-ing the game he would make a bit of a sacrifice to repay me. Good for Pete, he saw my point & paid me back in three months, & we didn't have a wrong word over the whole thing. Rather a funny thing, but when I first met Pete I disliked him, but then for that matter, I didn't like Howell either at first. Anyway, now I never make a deci-sion about a person at the first meeting, & reluctantly admit that one's intuition can be wrong.

Our two new foremen are due next month, but I still don't know definitely whether Ernie Perry is one of them. Have you heard any more yet?

I believe I mentioned that Bob Kraus told Mr. Howell before he went that his health was bad & he wanted to go home. Anyway, Mr. Howell arranged a meeting between Bob & the Works Director, Mr. Sitwell, who asked him if his health was all right would he want to stay on at his job.

Bob evidently said yes because an appointment was made
for him with Calcutta's best doctor. Unfortunately the
doctor was on leave in the hills, so Bob had to see his
"locum tenens," Dr. Mackay. Yesterday he had his overhaul & the verdict, well, his nerves are bad, he is properly
run down, he has some obscure stomach trouble, or as we
say, "he had got a bug," he is suffering from fatigue & his
teeth are bad. On top of this the Dr. says he doesn't drink
enough fluid. Bob said he didn't like water, so the Dr.
suggested beer & also suggested that he should drink five
bottles at work per day. On hearing this I immediately
tried to get an appointment with the same doctor, but so
far I have had no luck. Anyway, Bob has to go into a
Nursing Home for observation within a few days. He
came into my office this morning & his face was blue. He
certainly has got something wrong with him & the
sooner he goes home the better it will be for him.

Early this week, Bob & myself were requested to join
the European Association out here, by one of the directors, Mr. Irving. The fees are quite small & the idea is that
the Association represent & look after the interests of
Europeans in this country. Actually it is a useful organization, especially at the present time when we may get trouble with the Indians, therefore I sent in my application
right away.

Pete has been buying so much stuff lately that he just
doesn't know where to put it all, but an R.A.F. friend of his
arranged to send some of it home in a duty-free parcel.
Anyway, I too sent a python skin handbag in the same
parcel, & so when Pete gets home he will forward it on to
you. I don't know whether it is suitable or valuable. The
inside finish is not too good, but one night Pete & I & Mr.
& Mrs. Deefolts had been into Calcutta to the pictures &
after the show, as we were walking along Chowringhee

about midnight to get the car, we stopped to look at some handbags spread out on the pavement for sale. Pete, Mrs. Deefolts & myself each selected one & asked the price. The box-wallah told me 140 rupees, Mrs. Deefolts & Pete 90 rupees each. Really none of us wished to buy them, but just for fun I said 150 chips the lot, & after a bit of haggling, the Indian agreed. We still didn't want the things, so we turned away to find the car, & as a parting shot, I quoted a ridiculous figure & said "60 chips the lot." Just as we climbed into the station wagon the fellow caught us up with the three handbags in a parcel & said, "O.K. 60 cheeps." We nearly snatched his hand off, & Mrs. Deefolts said that never, even pre-war, could one buy snakeskin bags for that price. Anyway, Mam, it is yours if you can make any use of it.[38]

Last night we asked Alex Smith & Bob Embleton in for dinner, with a few beers & a game of snooker in Jessops' Club to start things off. Bob Embleton's wife has been in England about five months now & Bob is fed up & wants to go home for good too. It seems that the firm he works for, the "Indian Air Survey" in Dum Dum (Director Mr. Kemp, whom I have mentioned before) now the war is over have very little work because the R.A.F. have just about mapped all of India. Consequently the firm have no money to spend on new planes & Bob being both pilot & photographer, says that the planes they use are about twelve years old & the wings almost drop off in mid-air. Anyway, he is going to get out of the job & start again in England.

Incidentally, the Chinese General wants to take Alex & me to China when he goes home, for a three month's shooting trip this August. It is the chance of a lifetime & we would fly there & back, but three months is impossible for me, although Alex may go.

Hope everyone at home keeps fit. Mam, my health
is 100%.

Aug. 12th

Monday night with the rain swishing down off the palm
leaves & adding to the floods on the tennis court.

After a particularly hectic weekend I have decided to
stay in & knock off some back mail, also to climb under
the mosquito net at a reasonable hour before midnight,
instead of the usual 2 a.m.

As Ali Jinnah, on behalf of the Muslim League, has
declared war on the British & Congress from August
16th, the works will remain closed just in case of any trouble, so we all will have a quiet day in the bungalow & wish
Mr. Jinnah a short & unhappy life.

Everyone in the bungalow is once more fit & well,
although Jack is feeling homesick & has decided not to
bring his wife out here. He says things are too unsettled.
He should have read the papers before he decided to
come to India. It is perfectly obvious that 440 million
people will not remain a subject race with the lowest standard of living in the world. This country is due for a big
upheaval, politically & socially; too many Indians are
educated these days to be content to work under another
race, so inferior in numbers. The only solution is for those
same educated Indians to realize that, bad as the British
Govt. is, they rule better & more fairly than Bengalis,
Parsees, Marwaris, Congress & Muslims; there are too
many Indian Politicians with axes to grind.

A genuine effort on the part of the British to raise the standard of living here would restore their good name and immediately put Congress & Muslim League out of the running. Much as I detest the Indian Politicians, I admit that the Indian people don't get a fair deal. Personally, I think that the Indian problem is just another sign of the times & proof of the rotten state of the world.

The whole truth is that this world has not produced one man of any nationality who can be called a leader with a solution to the present state of affairs. Where are the modern equivalents of Aristotle, Archimedes, Plato, Confucius, Solomon, Buddha, Mahomet & the great thinkers of the past? The present shower think only of themselves or their immediate political parties. We have certainly sunk as low as it is possible; the brains which can produce the atom bomb with the sole purpose of destroying and blasting human beings off the earth in a most unpleasant manner, allowing millions of people to starve, do without homes & clothes & generally live in abject misery, while the world's top brains mess about with cosmic rays & heavier bombs, instead of chemicals for agriculture, etc....

Nevertheless, there is one small ray of hope. I read that Frank Sinatra had 'seen the light' & that thousands of Bobbysoxers hysterically sang hymns to tunes like "Scrub me Mama with a solid four" in company with the great swoon-crooner. After this "I've seen it all," as the Yanks say, & go my merry way without a care in the whole wide world.

I had a post card from Mr. & Mrs. Pete today with a wizard view of Newquay Cornwall, where they are still on holiday. Pete paints a glowing picture of England. Also I received a letter from an Engineer Sergeant of the British Army that I knew out here; he has been home several weeks now, & paints a picture which does not glow. He says he is glad to be back among his own people, but it is cold, there is no beer & it is cold, there are no cigarettes & it is cold. On top of all this, he says the climate is damned cold.

Incidentally, I have bought 2 pairs of stockings, sort of semi-fashioned artificial silk & I think they are about 8 or 8½. Anyway, I will send them wrapped in some magazines & if they aren't suitable, you can sell them or use them for dusters. There were some fully fashioned American stockings in the same shop, sunblonde, whatever shade that is. But the Joe who was selling them wanted 28 chips for them so I thought in the absence of an expert I wouldn't bother to make such a risky purchase.

The snap I have enclosed was taken in front of our bungalow after tiffin one Sunday. Left to right are Jack Simpson (the dysentery expert), Khan Bahadur, Kraus Shaheb the son of my bearer, who is very slightly darker than I am, and last in the line is a friend of Jack's who works for the Bengal Ingot Company in Calcutta. Just when this photograph was taken (by Bob's brother) I was saying to the big chap on the chair, "Dekho, wuh kala peti mén, ek-to chirja hai," which means in English, "watch the dicky-bird."

I have had a pleasant little letter from my bank today, stating that my account has been balanced by the sum of 4,259 rupees due TO me. Very heartening.

Well, Mam, best wishes to you all & the Vice Admiral weaving around the icebergs in the Arctic in a windjammer or something. I think I will paddle away downstairs for a bottle of beer & a couple of legs of chicken straight out of the "frig," before the gang come in from the Club; I daren't go to bed yet. If they want to make up a game of

solo, then out of bed I would come, whether I had had no
sleep for a week or not.
Keep fit and well.

Oct. 27th

Back once more to a life of working for my living, but
quite satisfied after a really good 3 weeks in Darjeeling. I
had quite a hectic journey back, on Saturday 19th. The
week before I left Singamari I had tried to book a berth
on the train to Calcutta, but was told that all trains were
booked up until the end of Oct.

This was no good to me, as I had already had a week
extra to my usual fortnight, so I reserved a seat on the railway bus down from Darjeeling & was prepared to take
my chance of getting onto the train at Siliguri. The day of
my departure arrived, & with it a cyclonic storm, lashing
rain, & I was absolutely frozen, even with my topcoat and
layers of pullovers. Anyway I boarded the bus at 4pm,
expecting to get into Siliguri at 6pm (the Calcutta train
left at 9pm) which left me 3 hours to bribe or wangle my
way on board.

The road was so bad, mists, landslides, muddy corners
where the bus slipped almost over the edge of the mountains, that I thought I had 'had it.' All the Indians on
board were violently sick, only an English Army Captain
& myself weren't ill, although neither of us felt too good.

We arrived at Siliguri at *20 minutes to 9 o'clock*, & I still
had to get a ticket. Finally, after being refused by Station

Masters, clerks, guards, engine drivers, etc., I swore in
Bengali, Urdu, Hindi, Tamil & Gurkhali at a junior clerk
who was so scared he sold me an inter-class ticket for 9
chips. Just as the train left I barged my way into a cattle
truck of a compartment with about 600 strong-smelling
cookes, thieves, goondahs, etc. & sat on my suitcase near
the door & kept my eyes open, & my hands on my watch
& money. I never slept a wink for the 400 mile trip to
Calcutta, & unfortunately I understood all the nasty
remarks in Bengali & Hindi directed at the sahibs in
general & me in particular.

That 11 hour journey was a nightmare & I was glad to
stretch my stiffened limbs on Scaldah Station.
Incidentally, Scaldah was complete bedlam. All the thousands of starving refugees from Noakhali were milling
round the platforms after fleeing from East Bengal where
they were being killed off in thousands. Getting back to
Dum Dum was quite a problem too. There was still a lot
of killing going on in Calcutta & I was fortunate in
getting a taxi driver who wasn't too scared to risk the trip.

On arriving at Dum Dum I found that we had already
moved into our new house in Post Office Road, spacious,
rambling & very old, but comfortable, cool & quite
decent. Since coming back I haven't had time to write a
single letter, so have a lot of back mail to catch up on.
There were 43 letters waiting for me on my return,
including one from D.A.F. Vincent with some snaps of
his daughter & my god daughter. There were some
bundles of magazines from you, thanks a lot. Incidentally
I re-use the gummed paper to send your stockings, etc.
back to you.

Everyone here reads the football news & we all join in
the enthusiasm over the Boro's fine start this season; all
the letters I get from people in England are full of accounts

of weekends at Ayresome Park, (wish I could see it).

The rains are now over & the weather is perfect, very welcome after the cold spell during my trip back from leave. This morning I went swimming at the Club (Jessops'), the first time in a month & found I couldn't cope after 4 lengths. I used to be able to swim a mile straight off (110 lengths). It will soon come back though, after a couple of days.

I have just read in the home papers where Cargo Fleet are asking for Platers. Bill Plews, the Middlesbrough lad who is in the Template Shop of Burn & Co. here, has packed up & leaves for England next month. He has a job ready to go to, & says that things are picking up in the Structural line at home.

I am enclosing some snaps, one on horseback outside the Gymkhana Club, Darjeeling. Left to right are Joan Farren, Jock Farren, Bob, Jean McIntosh & the local Sheriff. Just after this photograph was taken, Joan fell off her horse during a gallop down the path & smashed her chin into the ground. Fortunately, she soon recovered, although she had a nasty bruise on her jaw for the length of her stay. We all used to kid her, everytime we had a drink we would say, "Well, chin chin, Joan."

The other is a rather good snap of the house we just left, 18A Rajabagan. When we first arrived in India, Bob & I had a single room & bathroom upstairs in the house on the left, the rest of the building being a Drawing Office. Then we moved upstairs with Pete into the right-hand bungalow. The Drawing Office returned to Clive Street, Calcutta & Birchenough & his wife moved in on the left. The Birchenoughs went home on leave, Pete left & we moved into the house on the left with Alex Smith (Birch's father-in-law). The Birchenoughs have now returned from England & we have moved on into the top flat of No. 10 Post Office Road. We get around, don't we?

Anyway, life remains interesting and I enjoy every minute of it. Hope you do too. Best wishes to all at home & those in peril on the sea (Peril of being sea-sick). Keep fit.

Nov. 14th

For once I am spending a quiet evening at home, (everyone else is out) & I have been going through my drawers, cleaning out the old letters, etc. I find that I have 5000 rupees to my credit in the bank, with a Provident fund of 3000 rupees, so I am still solvent, or whatever one calls it. I also came across a bill from the Calcutta Swimming Club for my next year's contribution. It is just a year since I joined and, although several months have elapsed since I visited the Club, I have sent off a cheque for the next year; always somewhere to go to. Also found a slip of paper with the address: Colonel W.R.Ritchie, Mazbat P.O. District D'Arrang, Assam. I believe I told you the Colonel & his wife invited me up to their bungalow in the wilds for a 3 months' holiday; wish I could manage it, but little chance. Anyway, I shall write, they were damn nice people.

Jean McIntosh phoned me today, asking if Bob & I would like to go to a curfew dance & party at the 300 Club on Saturday. I suppose we will go if we can get transport. Jean says she is fed up with the types she meets in Calcutta & remembers the fun we had in Darjeeling.

They were good times, but one thing this country has taught me & that is to really enjoy & make the most of one's spare time. Sort of grab the chance with both hands, let one's hair down & don't waste a minute of any dance or party.

Whilst sorting out some of your old letters several things struck me that I failed to comment on before. First, you said that Harold Whittaker had left the Army, but didn't like Civvy Street. I was surprised, he didn't like the Army either. When a young man, he had a lot of enthusiasm & self-respect; but since getting that illness, he has sort of crumbled mentally. Second point, why did the British Govt. ration bread? Most people seem to have more than enough & B.U.s to spare.[39] Several letters from people at home mention this. I suspect it is a subtle political move with the general idea that we can now say to America, "We have now rationed the Staff of Life, what about you too, tightening your belts & contributing a little more food to the international pool?" In India we are rationed with bread, but except for a short period during the riots, we have never had to do without.

I am sorry you never received the snakeskin handbag; I sent it in a Services parcel through Paddy, the Irish Airman, to Pete, who was going to forward it to you. Incidentally, I have only had one letter from Pete's wife & a postcard from him. It seems that Pete left India with a few bills outstanding & some of his colleagues in the Mechanical Works asked me to mention these debts in my letters to him. I did, & I think Pete feels embarrassed by his debt, without wanting to pay it or mention it in his letters to me.

I still remain in rude & vigorous health, could sleep all day and all night if Jessops' would let me, smoke 50 cigarettes a day, drink beer when I can get it, take an interest

in my surroundings, & have no worries except being
bitten to hell by mosquitoes every night.

I still have a lot of enthusiasm for my work here, still
look out for a job in New Zealand (or South Africa. The
British Govt. seem to be transferring their capital &
influence to that country since India got their independence). I still prefer to be single rather than married, still
remain as black as ever, (I could pass as a Eurasian), and
remain in spirit and looks (so everyone says) 23 years of
age. Anyway, when I drift home in the year 1949, don't
expect me to be staid and serious.

I see that Arthur has been home again quite recently.
The service's life seems to be one long leave these days.
Not that they don't earn it. After a week or two on a 4x2
ship, tossing about in the cold Northern seas, I don't
expect Arthur finds life all beer and skittles. Also, if
Norman Miller is still in Palestine, I expect that the war is
still on as far as he, the Arabs & the Jews are concerned.
Same here in India. The trouble has now moved to Behar,
where the Hindus this time, being the majority community, are wiping the floor with the Mohommedans.

Quite a long time since I had any mail from you or
anyone in England. An Anglo Indian foreman of our
Press Shop, Brennan by name (you may remember I
visited his son & 3 daughters at school in Darjeeling) put
an advert in the Statesman for a nursemaid for his kids
(they are coming down next week for the cold weather
holidays). Brennan is a widower, & he advertised about a
month ago & is still receiving replies also written a month
ago. Everyday I go into his office & read through the
applications, & these letters really prove what a mess the
mails are in. Written anytime during the last month, &
coming from all over India, they are still arriving.
Anyway, I hope my letters get through to you. I still write

at least 2 a week & have sent 2 or 3 lots of snaps recently.

Jack Simpson's skin rash has cleared up now & he is looking quite fit, but Bob still doesn't look healthy. See that the 'Boro' slipped up badly by being beaten at home by Sunderland. The mornings are starting to get cool now, we will soon be wearing pullovers over our shirts, & Xmas is not very far away. Bob got a Xmas card today, which made me realize all of a sudden how close it is.

Best wishes to you all at home & good luck.

Dec. 6th

I have never seen any mention in your letters of postcards I sent from Darjeeling, to you and Violet, Derek Vincent, Ernie Cooper & several other people. I often wonder whether they were all lost. Also later, an air letter & a big letter containing a snap sent to the Vincents. Also, you should have received your stockings by now. The mail still seems very irregular, even if the letters do arrive.

My third Christmas away from home & according to preliminary reports and planning, this one is going to be the best of the lot, if Jinnah & Co. don't mess things up with riots & curfews, etc. A great deal depends on the talks now in progress in London. I still agree in principle that Indians should get their Independence & should govern themselves, but they can be such a lying, thieving, twisting, untrustworthy crowd, that I sometimes wonder whether we made a mistake in allowing them their free-dom. Just at present at work, we foremen have to make ourselves really unpleasant to make the men put their backs into the job. Today, for instance, I was taking a look round the back of some girders for some material when I almost fell over one of my portal crane slingmen. A Brahmin Hindu, Jaganath, asleep in the grass. I was as mad as hell & felt like kicking him, because these cranes are so busy, the yards being jammed up with material, loading wagons, etc. rivetters, welders, platers, all shouting for the crane, that I can't afford to have crane men loafing.

He immediately scrambled to his feet, thought out an excuse &, pointing to a small mark on his bare toe, said that he had cut his foot & was resting until the pain died away. I had several alternatives. I could swear at him until I was black in the face (I am, too), which wouldn't make the slightest impression on him. I could discharge him, losing a valuable man, because men are difficult to replace. I could suspend him for a week, which might have repercussions, him being a Brahmin & being able to stir up trouble, by saying that the slave driver sahib had forced him to leave the works when he was lying, half unconscious with pain.

Anyway, determined to teach him a lesson & make an example of him, I sympathised, suggested that he take three days off until his foot got better. He immediately said that it felt better already & he thought he could work. But I insisted that it might turn septic, and that I wouldn't like to lose such a valuable man, and that he should take his three days off. He left the works, not quite knowing whether I was "kidding", for three days' indirect suspension, while I had the satisfaction of knowing that losing three days' pay would make him more willing to work in future. This is a typical example of what we are up against.

Last Saturday night we went round to the Birchen-

oughs' for a bit of a "tamasha."⁴⁰ Jack, Bob & I, the
"Birches", E.B. Wilson (who provided his imported radiogram for the music), Arthur Dwyer & Mr. & Mrs. Farren
made up the party. The Radiogram is the same as the one
used at the Club on the night of the dance, with two, six
feet square loudspeakers on the lawn. The noise was terrific, like a brass band. I bet we woke the compound, too.

Bill Howell was sick and didn't turn up & Mr. Doak
was ill in bed, too. Alice Birchenough danced a really fine
"Ballet" on the lawn to some music from the "Nutcracker
Suite." She used to be very good at classic dancing. Also
we had a microphone fixed & had a "Round Robin,"
where everyone gets on the "mike" and gives a song; very
good, too.

We left about four in the a.m. & on reaching our
bungalow, found the chor-wallas had paid us a visit.
Chor-walla is Hindi for thief or burglar, and someone
who knew the ropes had found my key, opened all the
drawers in my room, opened my almirah, took out a small
wooden box and left me 80 chips worse off.

Jack's & Bob's rooms had been ransacked, but they
couldn't find anything missing. My fountain pen, cigarette case & lighter, chequebook, a silver watch, all lay in
the drawer, untouched, only my 80 rupees was missing
We came to the conclusion that it was one of our servants
who knew where we kept our money & also knew we
wouldn't be back until the early morning. He was pretty
shrewd, too, by not taking watches, etc. which could be
traced. Anyway, we decided it was a waste of time to
inform the police, & tried to solve the thing ourselves.
Bob had his wallet & 100 chips stolen when we stayed
with Alex Smith, he got all "steamed up", accused about
ten servants & spent almost every night for a week at the
police Thana, with no result. Therefore this time, know-

ing my India, I ignored the Police, interviewed the Jemadar,[41] two bearers, and the cook, accusing them of the theft (which they all denied), told them they would be sacked at the end of the month & have the 80 chips knocked off their combined wages. Also I sent my clerk along to the Post Office to find out from the Postmaster if any of them had sent more money home than usual. Now we just sit back and wait for things to develop.

Jimmy Bell's wife is now on the way out to this country. Whiteside has broken his contract with Jessops & got another job in Calcutta at three times his old salary. Jessops took legal advice to prevent him from going & were informed that the Agreement is not a valid Legal Document.

Enclosed is a snap (not very good) of our bungalow in Post Office Road, the wings are not visible in the snap. We occupy the upstairs flat & the roof goes a lot higher than shown. Incidentally, Bob did this print himself off the negative & got it all skew-wiff. Best wishes to you all & a very happy Xmas with plenty of grub.

Cheerio & love
Fred

1947

Jan. 2nd

Dear Mam,

Haven't had much time for writing letters lately, but have
had a marvellous time. Saturday the 28th I 'took off' the
morning and went into town to do some shopping.
Bought several shirts & socks & odds & ends. I had tiffin
at 12 noon & decided to visit some friends, a chap named
Oscar Taylor, an Australian who works in our Wagon
Works. Eventually he persuaded me to stay the weekend
with him, going to the cinema in the afternoon & a dance
at night.

Dec. 31st, as arranged, we all greeted the New Year at
the Burra Club. Jack Simpson said his dress suit wouldn't
fit him & refused to come along. Anyway, at 9pm, Bob &
I went round to the Birchenoughs' house in the
compound to pick up the rest of the party. Alex Smith,
Bob, & Arthur Dwyer & myself went in Alex's car, with
the Farrens, the Birchenoughs in Mac Ewing's car. Alex's
car has no hood, & the wind blowing made the journey
as cold as any in England. Arriving at the Burra Club at
9:30pm, we were joined by another chap & 3 girls to
complete our party.

At midnight, after supper & dancing, a Punjabi military band came onto the dance floor & played 'Auld Lang Syne' while everyone, especially the Scots, went mad. The Punjabis looked fine in their red coats, white breeches & puttees, & they played some fine Scots marches, ballads & reels. The European population of Calcutta is about 50% Scotch, so we danced jigs, eightsome reels, sword dances, & the air was full of whoops, hoch ayes & rolled "rrrs."

Birchenough & I kidded his wife & Alex Smith (his father-in-law) about visiting foreign festivals. We called it a Scotch Puja. Jack Ewing & Jock Farren are both Scotch too, & I come from near enough to the border to pass.

The only snag in the evening was, when getting into the cars to come home at 3 am, we found that Joan Farren's coat had been stolen out of Jack Ewing's car; with all doors & windows locked, too. But then, thieves in India are so clever and so abundant, it is impossible to live here without losing something to them.

Coming back to the compound we visited all the bungalows, first-footing.[42] Everyone agreed that I was the darkest person present, in fact they said I must be an Anglo-Indian, so I had to let in the New Year in most of the houses.

Jan. 5th

Second attempt at this letter. By the way, we three have had an argument with the local Bengali postmaster. He says that all air letter cards written by one civilian to another are not accepted as air mail, but will be sent as sea mail. He says that 6 anna air letter cards are a military concession & either the sender or the receiver must be military. Anyway, we did not agree and are making inquiries about it, & have threatened to break his neck if he sends any of our air letter cards sea mail. If you are receiving my air letters late, this is probably the reason. I still get your mail regularly including the magazines, & in reply to your question about receiving Violet's second attempt at poetry, I did, & replied to it the same day. So if you didn't get my letter, *that* must be lost.

Incidentally, I'm beginning to realize why the British have such a name and place in the world & why they have held on to their Empire for so long. I can imagine foreigners not understanding us. Take for instance this country: the Hindus don't want us, the Muslims are saying 'Quit India,' there has been rioting & massacres,& a European's life is anything but safe. Everyone said they were going to get out of it before the shooting started & they had no intention of staying here. But Birchenough returned *&* brought his wife. Doak returned & brought his wife *&* kids. Jim Bell has just brought out his wife. Mr. Howell brought his wife & daughters back from Ootacamund (which he swore he would never do). Jack Ewing's wife is on the way out. Joan Farren is not going home now, & is going to bring up her child in this country. Jack Simpson is talking about bringing his wife out, and Alex Smith is going home on leave & intends to bring his wife back with him.

It just doesn't make sense. I wouldn't say they were brave, they just can't be bothered to run away & adapt themselves to new conditions of living. It takes more than a riot or civil war to stir up a Britisher. He just carries on as usual. Actually, I think this is a real virtue in these times, when people refuse to be upset or disturbed by all the rumours which threaten us. After all, if we thought of what might happen to us, life wouldn't be worth living & we would be old people at 20 years of age. The very fact that Britishers carry on normally, tends to create an air of security & stability, & quietens the fears of the Indians themselves.

By the way, Alex Smith has packed in his job with Burn
& Co., is going home for a short leave, & then is going
into partnership with a friend of his out here. Alex has
several irons in the fire & is a director of several small
companies. He, too, was at the Howell's party last night,
which I described in an air letter. Sheila & Joan Howell
are tremendously big girls, Joan being very well built, as
well as being tall. With semi-high heeled shoes on, she
towers over me. I often wish I wasn't so small. Being tall
is a very definite advantage. Tonight the mosquitoes are
out in force. It being the coldest month of the year,
January is the worst for 'mossies,' although it is not a
malaria month. I find that undiluted Dettol keeps them
away somewhat, but they still *get* me.

Bob is developing some films we took at the childrens'
Xmas party tonight, so if they come out all right, I will
send you some.

Jack is walking around in a purple dressing gown & is
opening a bottle of beer, nice work.

Best wishes to you all.

Jan. 27th

Just can't get down to letter writing lately, always something or someone turns up to divert my attention.

Last Saturday, after an extremely busy & tiring morning at work, I reached the bungalow with the intention of
going to bed for the weekend. I had a particularly lousy
cold due to the sudden changes of temperature during
Bengal's cold season. After the heat of the day, around

5pm as the sun goes down so does the thermometer
(about a degree every minute & some nights are quite
warm when we go to bed, until around 4am when the
cold, fog, dew, etc. descends & the atmosphere changes in
5 minutes, sub-tropical to near Arctic).

Anyway, after tiffin I threw open my jill-mill windows,
dragged my bed into the sun & was just going to haul my
weary limbs onto the sheets for a solid 50 hours' sleep,
when the bearer came in & announced the arrival of
Corporal Jamieson. I therefore had to forfeit my sleep.
I had sent a letter to Maurice telling him not to come
down, as I was going out to dinner on Saturday, but he
told me (as he sat on the bed with a bottle of beer) that
my letter didn't arrive.

We sat and talked until tea time, & as I felt better by
this time, Bob & I dressed in our evening suits to be ready
for the car coming at 6pm. Jack Simpson had nothing to
do, so I fixed Maurice up with shorts & tennis shoes, & he
& Jack went down into the compound to play badminton
with the Mitchells downstairs.

At 6pm Jack Ewing & Arthur Dwyer arrived in the car
to take us into Calcutta. On arrival at Freemasons' Hall in
Park Street, I had a couple of pegs of whiskey & felt quite
a lot better.

After the meeting, at the Banquet, all the visitors had to
reply to the visitors' toast with a speech, (which I am
never very keen on) so this time I had the good excuse of a
cold, and dug Bob in the ribs & he had to get on his feet &
say his piece. It's an ill wind that blows nobody any good.

About 20 of Jessops' people were at the meeting,
including Johnny High, a Scotsman working in the
Wholsale Dept. at Clive St. Johnny is a real good guy, is
henpecked, has a beautiful wife & 2 nice kids. He is small-
ish, wears glasses & a perpetual worried look. It seems

that Johnny had been to a fairly hectic Lodge meeting and
his wife Barbara said, "Ok, go ahead, enjoy yourself. I
shall go out with a couple of the boys." Anyway, after our
dinner, as we climbed into Jack's car Johnny said, "What
about coming round to my place for a drink?" He knew
his wife wouldn't go out without him, but he was scared
to go home alone, because his wife was sure to chew his
ears off.

So we agreed to go along as sort of moral support for
Johnny, & to prevent any bloodshed. When we arrived at
his flat, his wife was out & Johnny's car was missing from
the garage.

We had a few beers, Johnny took our photographs
with his new camera, & we talked of shikar, work, India &
henpecked husbands. Midnight passed. We had a few
more beers. 1am passed (& some more beers). 2am, &
then, just as we had decided to leave for Dum Dum, we
heard a car come into the compound. The door opened
and Barbara came in, evening dress, fur coat, etc. & looking as if she had had a really good time. Johnny's usual
worried frown was deeper, & he was talking with a bit of a
limp by this time.

The following half hour's conversation amused me
more than a cinema comedy, the conversation going
something like this:

Barbara "Enjoy yourself, John?"
Johnny "Yes, darling. Where have you been?"
Barbara "Enjoying myself, John."
Johnny "But, darling, where *have* you been?"
Barbara "I've been out with the most attractive fellow.
We danced tangos all night."
Johnny "But darling, where *have* you been?"
Barbara "I'm not telling you, John, but let me know

when your next Lodge meeting is, I'm going out dancing
again."

We had already invited Johnny to our next Dum Dum
Meeting, but he has declined the invitation now (I
wonder why?).

On Sunday (after a troubled sleep with thousands of
mosquitoes in the dining room, as Maurice was in my
bed) we arose late & after tiffin, played badminton.
Incidentally, Maurice & Jack had a good night at the Club
on Saturday. Most of the crowd came in & Maurice got
on fine with them. Actually he had only been in bed half
an hour when we came in at 4am. After our badminton &
tea on the veranda, I had decided to knock off a couple of
letters when a note came round from Jock Ewing asking if
I would like to play off our billiard handicap semi-final.
I agreed, so we all drifted round to the Club & I played
Jock. I had a 50 back handicap and Jock was scratch, so
I would have had to play unusually well to beat him.
Anyway, Jock won by 15 & I joined the ranks of the also
rans.

As Maurice had to catch the last bus at 9pm, we left &
walked to the main road. On the way he told me he was
leaving shortly for Rawalpindi, & eventually the Battalion
was moving on to Syria.

The main road bus stop is a lonely, deserted place, a
few lights in the distance, not even any Indians about, &
with the jungle behind us & the wails of the jackals.
Anyway, as the bus (with Maurice aboard) rattled away
down the dark road, I stood for a while to sort of really
appreciate the scene (scene is hardly the word I require).
I wanted to sort of get the event settled in the right
perspective.

The silence; the loneliness, except for the hum of

insects & the jackals; myself, thousands of miles from
Ormesby; also Maurice bumping into me at the other
side of the world (the last time we met in England,
neither of us thinking that we should one day meet again
in Dum Dum). Now he is off to Syria & I may go
anywhere from here. Probably the next time I see him will
be in the Odeon, or at the Village Hall Dance.

Soon I was back among the lights & laughter of the
Club, to find that Mr. & Mrs. Doak had arrived. After a
couple of hours they said goodnight & left & we were just
leaving when Mrs. Doak came back on her own & asked
us if we would like to come round to her place for sandwiches & beer. Naturally we accepted, & arrived at the
Doaks' at 11pm. I made sandwiches, Jock Ewing & Dwyer
supplied cold pork & potatoes, Mrs. Doak made coffee,
Bob opened the beer, & Jack looked after the radiogram.

We had a really good party until 4 o'clock in the morning. Mrs. Doak is a really good sport & we played darts,
danced, played liars' dice & ate until we nearly 'bust.'
Most of the people in this world are out for themselves,
with no thought for others, & in self-defence, one has to,
well, look after oneself, because sooner or later most of
the people one knows & trusts let one down. Mrs. Doak
is a woman in a million, a real tonic to meet. As she left
the Club, she thought of we three bachelors going home
with no mem sahib's company, to a badly cooked meal
probably, and immediately she turned back to bring us
round to her bungalow.

Hope you are all fit, well & happy. Best wishes to you
all & Love.

Feb. 2nd

After a couple of weeks of staying in Dum Dum, yesterday we 'beat it up' in Calcutta. The whole thing was sort
of decided on the spur of the moment & up to 9:30pm on
Saturday evening I didn't know I was going to town. We
left work as usual at tiffin time & after lunch, Jack, Bob &
I all decided to hit the pillow for a few hours, being tired
out after a particularly busy week of work.

I awakened at 4:30pm with the arrival of the postman
with a parcel from Maurice, containing some gym shoes,
which he had promised to send. After tea we went down
into the compound for badminton & to try out my new
shoes. There was quite a crowd downstairs, & we played
until 9pm under the electric arc lights we have fixed up.

We had decided to go round to the Club later, there is
usually a crowd there on Saturday night, & we were all
getting changed. Actually, I was standing under the
shower when the bathroom door burst open & there was
Arthur Dwyer, resplendent in evening dress. He said,
"Come on, you so & sos, get your tuxedos on. We are
going into town for some nice, quiet fun, & I've
borrowed Jock Ewing's car for the occasion." Well, once
Arthur gets an idea in his head, there is no altering it, so
Bob & I got dressed up, (Jack wouldn't come) & we set
off for town at 10pm.

On the way, we called at Cossipore to see if some
friends of Arthur's (Mr. & Mrs. Gallagher from
Cawnpore & old nieghbours of Arthur's when he lived
there) would come with us. Mrs. Gallagher had already

gone to bed, so her husband said it was off as far as they were concerned, so we set off alone.

Arriving at the Burra Club, I soon lost both Arthur & Bob & found myself at a table with a Nepali Major General. I don't quite know how I came to be introduced to him. Anyway, his name was Krisha Shum Shere Jung Bahadur Rama Thapa, which I could almost have guessed, as all the wealthy Nepalis have the Shum Shere Jung Bahadur bit in the middle. Like all Nepalis, he had a round, good-natured face & smiled continuously. He told me that he left Military College as a young officer, was sent to Burma & got a Jap bullet through his lung on the first day in the front line. After recovery he was sent back & during his first week in Burma again, he got mixed up with a bomb & as he said with a smile, "The doctor have to cut my leg from here." He drank his Scotch neat, had a head, neck, shoulders & chest like a bull, and after excusing himself, "Please, you let me go now, my wife she is seek," he limped toward the exit on his tin leg. I felt sorry for such a young chap who took his misfortune so easily.

By this time I hadn't had a dance, so I decided to drift round & see 'what the score was,' & coming to a table occupied by a young Scot I had met before, (he is an electrical engineer about my age), I danced with his partner, but left them feeling rather disturbed, because he mentioned that his firm have just made him a monthly grant of Rupees 1300 for living & as an entertainments allowance, apart from his ordinary salary. I thought, by hell, his entertainments allowance is more than my full salary.

But I promptly forgot about it when the cabaret & floor show came on, & I considered that I am not exactly a pauper myself. I stood beside a pillar & watched the

show. The dancing, an old fashioned minuet danced in
costume, was very good. The music was the 'Moonlight
Sonata' played by four old Mezzo Soprano types sawing
on cellos & violins, but the music was very good actually.
The lights had just come on again when someone
behind me said, "Hello, Fred. Come & sit down. How
did you get here?" It was Joan Farren, & instead of rusti-
cating in Dum Dum as I thought, she & Jack were having
a night out in town too. I sat down with their party &
Joan introduced me all round: Mr. Hebel, Doctor Konek,
Francesca Szlabo, Humperdincks & Vinegarteners,
Blozeks & Blinkerstrassers. They were all Hungarians,
& a nicer shower of people you couldn't hope to meet.
Homely but intelligent, friendly & happy, but what
struck me most was their perfect manners. Doctor Konek
said, "So, you are a padchelor. I am a padchelor too, bud I
vish I vas marrie't." He had been educated in America.
    The next dance was an old-fashioned waltz, so I danced
with Francesca Szlabo, a typical Hungarian: blonde hair,
straight, with a bun at the back, & an accent one could cut
with a knife, but very pleasant to listen to. She called me
Mr. Trumboldt, & asked me, "h'if I cudt re-ferss."
    I left the party to find the lads & came across Bob &
Arthur sitting on high stools at the bar with a crowd of
fellows they knew. I said, "V'ere half you p'een, poys?"
Dammit, those Hungarians had me talking like that now.
Anyway, we stayed until the finish & arrived back at Dum
Dum at 4 this morning after a welcome change from the
usual routine.
    An item of news which I don't know whether I
mentioned before, Bob Embleton, an old Dum Dum
friend of ours, has been awarded the M.B.E. or the O.B.E.,
I'm not sure which, for meretorious service to the British
Empire. Bob is a photographer & pilot of the Indian Air

Survey & last year he went on rather a secret air survey of Tibet & the Himalayas, so I suspect he got his award for this job.

The Calcutta Tramways are still on strike, & a general strike of all industry & services on Feb. 5th for one day (although I think the Works will carry on that day), has been scheduled by unions & the workers. India still remains as unsettled as ever, anything may happen, so by next year we might be living in England, or Burma, India or New Zealand. I still keep my eyes open & watch political developments in this country. I see from the papers that the British Govt. have decided to evacuate all non-military personnel from Palestine. Who knows? The same thing may happen here one day.

Burn & Co. have started a new system of wage & salary grading for their staff. This is the reason that Alex Smith resigned. There are four grades: Junior Lower, Junior Upper, Senior Lower, & Senior Upper. The new green assistants straight from College or out from England are classed as Junior Lower, & so on, up to managers etc. at the top. As we young fellows came out when foremen were in short supply, we had "greatness thrust upon us." In other words, we were running a full department, when, under normal conditions, we would still be learning the language, methods, etc. for at least 2 years, followed by 3 years as ordinary foremen, with our present responsibility coming during our second contract.

Therefore, we may be much better off under this salary grading & get paid for the job we are doing, instead of getting a first contract salary. Alex Smith left Burn & Co. because, under the grading he was entitled to less than he is getting now on his next contract. Incidentally, we met him at a Lodge meeting the other night and brought him round to our place for a couple of beers. He has got "several irons in the fire," so after 3 months' holiday in England, he will return to India to take up another manager's job for an Indian firm at about 3500 chips a month (very nice too).

Well that's all for now. Hope everyone at home is well, working & happy. When are Arthur & Violet going to get married? They are getting old now.

Feb. 13th

Have just remembered that both Arthur & Violet have a birthday during this month, so this letter contains my late, but nonetheless sincere wishes for their future, with 'many happy returns,' although they have both reached a ripe old age now, Violet being 24 or 25 & Arthur 21, I think.

Work still occupies most of my time, & like most other people, I thought that after the end of the war, I would be able to 'rest on my oars' a bit, but here we are busier than ever before. By accounts in recent papers, things aren't going too well in Britain either: cuts in electric power & coal, with the temperature 30° below freezing. Most of the reports blame the present Government, & although I still remain a Socialist (not a Communist or Tory), I think that Shinwell has made a mess of his job & should hand over to someone more competent. Shinwell should definitely have seen this coal crisis coming & taken steps to prevent it or at least informed the Public of what to expect.

We, too, have our labour problems. The Calcutta

Tramways are still on strike, also the Port Commissioners, while here at Dum Dum the workers of the Gramophone Company went out on strike & immediately were granted a 50% increase of Dearness Allowance by the firm, so they are back at work today. As they got their requests granted so easily, we can expect trouble in Jessop's, which personally I would welcome to get the air cleared. The men are very dissatisfied & are not working as they should while Government restriction of overtime puts the Staff to a lot of trouble to finish off urgent work & repairs. My fabrication costs are 'all to hell' too, every job being more expensive to make than is estimated (although I suspect that Jessop's are still making a lot of money). As I have said before, foremen had to be engineers when we first came to this country, but now we have to be 'ruddy' diplomats, too.

Last weekend we three went into town for dinner with the Jimmy Bells. I mentioned in a previous letter that Jimmy had been given his marching orders by the firm, not because of incompetence, but because he didn't see eye to eye with E.B. Wilson. He and his wife are staying at a hotel in town & most of the residents are Armenians or Anglo-Burmese. Mrs. Bell is a youngish, fresh-faced blonde, with an accent you can cut with a knife. A good sport, she doesn't seem to be bothered by the fact that, although she has sold her home in Scotland, she now has to return & start again, & she likes India too. We had a good night & saw a film at the Lighthouse Cinema, John Garfield in "Nobody Lives Forever."

Sunday, 16th
After a morning in bed we have just had tiffin, a fairly hot chicken curry, something that we never eat, even after 3 years in the country. Today we had curry for Jack's

benefit, the first time he has had it in his life.

The morning in bed was the result of last night's Installation banquet of our Lodge. After the meeting, we all climbed into our cars & set off for the Cossipore Club for the dinner. The night was hot & still, in fact we have been having freak hot weather for February. Anyway, I managed to pack seven courses away under my stiff shirt. I sat between Alex Smith (now living in Calcutta) & a German professor named Budzredauski, drinking Scotch Whiskeydauski. The Professor was a real long haired type, but later he entertained us at the piano. He was a good musician. I was introduced to him by a mutual friend, Bill Starkmann, an Austrian who has just taken out British Naturalization papers. Bill works at the Gramophone Company.

As usual the Yorkshiremen & the Scots kept the party going. One Yorkshireman, Laveck, a Lieut. Colonel in the R.E.M.E. & dressed in the old army dress suit, dark blue, tight pants with a red stripe, & a high collar, made a really good after dinner speech. As a visitor, he thanked us for our hospitality. He said he had been around, & our hospitality was second to none, except for a brief stay of his in a friendly little jail in the United Provinces.

Next Saturday is our Lodge Annual Ball, to be held at the Cossipore Club. I have written to Maurice Jamieson asking him to come down & we will see if we can fix him up with an old dress suit, but he has to find his own partner. I almost forgot to mention it, but during the dinner the atmosphere became warmer & warmer, until after a terrific display of lightning the storm broke, just like the monsoon, & we drove home in pouring rain. Today the skies are grey, the atmosphere cool, with no wind, in fact, ideal for badminton, so when my curry has settled, I am going down into the compound for a game.

I note from your last letters that Fred Barker is now living in Dew Lane, that Jack Sheffield is back at Cargo Fleet, & that Norman Miller is back home. I don't suppose he is sorry to leave Palestine.

Everyday we get Junkers planes (3 engined) flying over Dum Dum, conveying French troops to French Indo China. There is still a war on in that section, remember, & fighting continues in China, too.

Since Mrs. Doak arrived in this country with her 2 kids, they have had some bad luck. Mr. Doak used to hit the bottle pretty hard when he lived on his own, & since his wife returned, he let up a bit, but he got blood pressure or something, so has to take things easy. Then both the kids were sick & when they did get the boy off to school in Calcutta, the car he was travelling in was stoned by gangs of goondahs during a demonstration, so he hasn't been to school since.

Hope you all keep fit at home during the cold snap. I can't even imagine the cold of Tees-side now, I've been among the heat for so long (& still like it). Our brief winter is almost over & still Mr. Howell comes into work with tweed coat, collar & tie, etc. He has very thin blood; in fact the Indians stand the cold better than he does. The poorer class of cookes only possess one thin cotton dhoti & a raggy shirt, and go around barefooted. No wonder Bill Howell won't spend his leave in England, the climate would kill him. He is a most peculiar chap. His daughters, Joan 17 & Sheila almost 21, have never been to a dance, never leave Dum Dum except for a very occasional trip into Calcutta, & are really kept tied down worse than any girls of Victorian days. Incidentally, they are both about 5'10" or 5'11" tall.

Best wishes to you & all the gang. I haven't had any

reply to my last letter to the Vincents, sent months ago.
Probably he is too busy at his council meetings.

Mar. 9th

Sunday night, & I am sitting at my bedroom desk with the
fan slowly turning above me. The night is warm but, as
usual in March, there is a cool breeze blowing, so I have
opened all my jill-mill windows, allowing the breeze to
enter with millions of mosquitoes too. I have just been
rubbing Dettol on my arms & ankles to keep them from
biting. It seems fairly successful.

   Our house, large & rambling as it is, has only one glass
window & that is in my bathroom. All other windows are
jill-mills, that is, like a double door with a Venetian blind
contraption which can be raised or lowered, to keep out
the sun but let in the air.

   We have been swimming all day & I am regaining
my usual copper skin, although the scorching my hide
received when I was on leave at Gopalpur has left my body
fairly brown, normally, even in winter.

   We have had a young soldier staying with us this weekend. He was a friend of Bob's brothers & has visited us
once before. Last night we all attended the Jessops' dance
at the Club. A really good night, with a crowd coming by
bus from Calcutta (the Head Office staff). The Howells
were there, the girls all lashed up in long frocks; Joan told
me it was her first real dance, & I believed her because I
took her round in an old-fashioned waltz. She is taller &

heavier than I am & dances like a frightened horse, (the
result of living a secluded life). Jack Simpson was in charge
of the bar, & Bill Howell put away more than his share of
whiskey, & was dancing with all the beauties, while Mrs.
Howell watched. Anyway, she still wears the pants in that
outfit, & when she said, "Time to go home," away home the
family went, whether they wanted to go or not.

Unfortunately the Doaks could not attend. Mrs. Doak is
out of the Nursing Home, but is still in bed. Jock Ewing's
wife is on the way out so he is taking things easy & did not
turn up. And Mrs. Farren isn't built for dancing at present,
so they, too, were absent.

Last Friday was the Hindu Puja of Doljatra & a holiday
for us. We & the Farrens booked the Works' car & travelled
to Calcutta, where we spent the day at the Calcutta
Swimming Club. My first visit for about six months, but
the Club is still one of the best places in town. I was
surprised at the number of people I met that I knew. Of
course everyone was on holiday. I was also surprised to find
that after one length of the outside pool, I had "had it," but
if the weather remains as hot as at present, I shall soon
regain my old style.

After 5pm we left the Club, (all looking very sunburnt),
& went to the first performance of "Notorious," with Cary
Grant & Ingrid Bergman, at the lighthouse.

Mar. 11th

Tiffin time. Have just had some magazines from you &
an air letter. I note that wintry conditions still remain & my
Littlewoods coupon is 'scrubbed' for another week.[43]

I have just been picking the billiards & snooker team to
play at Cossipore Club on Thursday. This is part of my job
as billiards member on the committee. Also this morning,
got a phone call from Jock Ewing to say that I am playing in
the Jardine Cup Golf Competition Sunday the 23rd at

Tollygunje. This is my debut in golfing circles, so someone should get a good laugh, probably me.

Mar. 12th
Just received your letter with enclosed cuttings of
Burnley-Boro goal. You will probably have a letter of
mine by now, where I mention that the Boro would win
the cup (in my opinion) if they beat Burnley at Burnley.
Although Burnley are only a 2nd Division team, on their
own ground they can beat any 1st Division team, because
they play more robust football. Your enclosed cuttings
prove this; the instant that Cumming fumbled the ball
after the free kick, he had a Burnley man standing on his
face & another sitting on him. I know the style, having
played with & against 1st & 2nd Division professional
footballers. Incidentally, Bob, Jack & I all backed Burnley
to win. It seems to me that, as usual, the Boro have 3 or 4
brilliant footballers in the side & the rest are just passengers.
    I see from today's papers that questions are being asked
in Parliament about evacuating British European subjects
from this country in 1948 when we hand over to the
Indians.
    Am enclosing a cutting re launching of the floating
dock which Jessops partly built. This was the first job I
worked on in this country, & so I am pleased to see that it
went together o.k., even the four portal cranes running
on the top, which gave us a lot of trouble during fabrication.
    In one of the recent "Illustrateds" was an article on
Badminton, in which we were interested. It included a
statement to the effect that the game originated in India,
but was no longer popular & was seldom played. As soon
as Bob read it he sat down & wrote a letter to the editor

questioning the writer's opinion & saying that in his
(Bob's) opinion, Badminton is *the* most popular game in
this country. Anyway, in the next issue you may read it
yourself if they publish the letter.

Work still remains very strenuous, with everyone rushing around, but not much output. Mr. Howell spends
most of his time in the office, and hardly knows what is
happening in the shops, & consequently knows less & less
of the little snags of production. As far as he is concerned,
a job is a drawing & all he wants is output. He never
comes in contact with the labour & therefore has very
little idea of how tactful we have to be in dealing with the
men in these unsettled times. He is cutting the mens'
wages right & left, & leaving the explaining to us to do, &
we have to get the work out of these same men, too.

For any young man (to complete his education), I
would suggest three years of life in a chummery as we live.
It certainly did Peter Page a lot of good, & Jack Simpson
too. He is quite a good sport now. He & Bob used to
be a real pair of groaners. This life tends to knock off the
rough edges or smooth out the bad points in one's character. For instance, we three go out to the Club, & the
servants put our dinner on the stove in the cookhouse.
Two of us come home at 10pm & have dinner and as most
people, are pretty thoughtless. The average person would
not bother to replace the third man's dinner on the stove,
or put some more water on to boil for the other chaps'
tea. But in a chummery, one just has to toe the line. We
learn tolerance too: perhaps having just got nicely off to
sleep at night, one of the other guys might drag you out
of bed to make up a game of snooker at the Club. One just
has to tolerate it & learn to 'muck in.' Of course, three
years of this life is enough. Without a woman around the
house things get a bit tedious at times.

Hope you all remain as fit as I am. Best wishes to all at home & to the gang.

Mar. 16th

Sunday morning, with a blue sky, hot sun & a strong breeze blowing. In fact, ideal weather & very different from what you are experiencing in England just now. From what I read in the papers, & see in the film news reels, the cold spell in the British Isles has beaten all records for longevity & severity. I should imagine the weather is most unpleasant.

India is now very rapidly moving towards either chaos, or a new way of life, & we (the Europeans) are coming to the conclusion that within the next two years we will all have to leave. Not that the Free Indian Govt. or the Industrialists, or the educated Indians or the cooke classes want us to leave. On the contrary, they all want us to stay, realizing that this country cannot supply all her demands for technicians, & in the interests of the country, Industry must be kept running. The Indian who will cause all the trouble is the Bengali babu class, the half-educated caste conscious, biased individual who fills the country's clerical posts; the young student gang that leads the processions & is the direct cause & instigator of all the riots, the political & antiracial unrest. This is the type of Indian who will make life very unpleasant for the British who intend to remain here. Possibly, for the European who can "stick it" there will be plenty of good jobs, because the capitalist class will make working here as attractive as possible, just to hold onto their administrative staff. But outside of work, the European will be insulted & will generally have a rough time.

The other night, while attending a Lodge dinner, I was seated next to a Mr. Webber, a recording engineer from the Gramophone Company. I knew him slightly, he came out with Peter Page, got a dose of dysentery & after emetine injections which somehow went wrong, he lost the use of his legs & one arm. He was seriously ill for a year, & I met him in Darjeeling where he could walk round with the aid of a stick. Today he is still very thin & lame, but manages to get around.

He told me that in 1936 he had to be evacuated from Barcelona, because of the Spanish war. From there he went to Germany & had to be evacuated [again] just before war broke out. Then he got this job in India after two and a half years at Hayes, Middlesex, & now he says that he might also be evacuated from India in two years' time (or less). Anyway, whatever happens, there is sure to be plenty of variety & happenings of interest.

Just at present there is a civil war in progress in the Punjab & Lahore, & in Calcutta area unrest & strikes continue. Incidentally, the Calcutta Tramways employees are still on strike, since the middle of January, with no hope of any settlement to the dispute, so far. Actually the trams are to Calcutta what the Underground is to London, so you have some idea of the travelling inconvenience for the ordinary Indian workman here during the last two months.

Mar. 19th
Sorry I have to make so many attempts to finish my letters, but [because] we can't get hold of any air letters

now, I can't sit down at tiffin time & send you a letter, so I have to write a long one in installments.

Mr. Howell went to Delhi by air yesterday, to see some sample passenger coaches similar to those that we will make. He is returning later this week, also by air. Air travel is unrestricted in India now, no controls & no priorities. This morning I had a letter from Burkinshaw, one of the Directors of Jessop's, informing me that I have been insured for air travel with the New Zealand Insurance Society, in the event of my having to travel by air for Jessops on business. Last year I half-expected having to go to Burma during the erection of Myitnge (Mingee) Bridge, which we built here. I mentioned the job in previous letters, where the site engineers were stumped, they couldn't find a way to erect the centre spans (six spans altogether) in midstream. Jessops solved the problem by temporarily joining the six spans together & pushing them out on rollers. Fortunately the site engineers did as we proposed & the bridge is now in use.

This Monday & Tuesday have been real scorchers. We went straight to the Club after work at 5pm, & cooled off in the swimming pool, with tea under the palm trees, very refreshing. Late last night a terrific gale blew up. Today was dull, cool & gusty, & this evening at tea-time, another gale arrived without any warning & almost blew us away. By reports in the papers, a severe earthquake was reported with the epicentre somewhere in the Himalayas about 900 miles from Calcutta, so these tremors probably started the movement of air & caused the gales.

Life remains fairly quiet for we three bachelors. Too hot for badminton, the Birchenoughs are hard up & are staying indoors, Jock Ewing is taking things easy until his wife arrives, Mrs. Doak is still recuperating, the Farrens have naturally dropped out of Dum Dum social life, & Mr. Howell is away. So, until Sunday, when we all meet for the Golf Tournament, we are all living a secluded life.

I can imagine the feelings of some of the old British residents here in India as they watch the British leaving the country. After all, this place is absolutely steeped in tradition, all the houses and buildings have their history dating from Clive's day[44]. In our Lodge we have a huge table which was used as an operating bench by the British surgeons during the Indian Mutiny. Instead of electric fans, we have the old pull-punkahs, a suspended frame with hanging coconut mats which are pulled by a coolie with a rope, causing a draught. The old Dum Dum Ammunition Factory where they ring a bell & hoist the Union Jack everyday, as they did when it was a military fort protecting the East India Company property. All these places are rapidly being taken over by Indians, although, we have been in this country for so long that British influence, tradition & custom will, to some extent, remain.

The other day I was talking to one of the Heads of the I.S.D. An Indian from Sind named Nathanie, he said he was sorry the British were going in 1948, but comforted himself with the thought that Nehru & Company would be pleased to hand India back again after a couple of years of muddle, as he (Nathanie) thinks they will get.

Personally, I will be sorry too when India leaves the British Empire, but every man has the right to choose his own Government & policy, so our Labour Govt. are doing the correct thing in handing over.

Hope you all keep well & the thaw sets in soon, with Spring, more food, & more of everything for you.

Mar. 28th

Friday evening & I am just recuperating after a strenuous day in the sun. The temperature reached 100 degrees outside (about 97° in the shade). Three of my rivetters on metre gauge wagon floor plates collapsed with the heat. I drift around wearing a floppy sombrero (the topee is now obsolete),[45] shirt, shorts, ankle socks & dark glasses, with the sweat pouring down my face, neck & legs & oozing through my shoe lace holes. (How does it feel to be cold?)

Rioting has once more broken out in Calcutta, although so far the fighting is confined to only a few districts. However, the Hindus & Muslims still break each others' heads with all the old zest & careless abandon. There must be over 2000 casualties now. Fighting in the Punjab is not as severe, but they are still putting up a good show in spite of the patrolling of 20,000 troops.

This surely is a hell of a country & I think very bitterly of the mess caused by British rule in India. If only we had had one sensible Government in the old days, Indians would now have been our friends & this country would have been a real jewel of the Empire with tremendous advantages both to Indians & British. At present, the only thing we can do is get out & stay out, & the loss is *ours*.

At tiffin time I was shaving (I had intended to leave my beard for a few days, but the sweat & bristles made my face sore). Anyway, as I scraped away, I looked out of the bedroom window and could see a bullock cart passing.

The nearside bullock had almost "had it" with the
extreme heat, the overloaded cart, the wooden yoke
biting deep into the open sores on the animal's neck, the
bumpy road. This is India & all the beasts of burden are
treated like this. The ruddy so & so (there is only one
name for a bullock cart driver & it is very, very profane)
driving the cart was evidently in a hurry & he beat the
bullock over the head & eyes as hard as he could go with a
thick stick. The animal's tail was disjointed, broken in six
or seven places where he had twisted it. Anyway, I leaned
out the window & called him all the "sons of guns" I
could manage in Hindi & Bengali. He was rather
impressed, but as soon as he was at safe distance he laid on
with his stick again. All this is just to give you some idea
of the type the ordinary Indian can be, cruel to a point the
European mind can't grasp. This is the man that is now
going to govern himself; given the chance, he would treat
me like his bullock; but it is too late for anything to be
done to change his mentality. The system is wrong, no
education, etc. The only way was to bring up the young
generation to think properly years ago. We were too busy
exploiting the Indians to think of helping them, hence we
have 440 million people who hate us, hate each other &
are ripe for a civil war.

Of course, the obvious thing to do is for the British to
hang on in the country, prevent any riots & start again.
But it is too late, our name stinks here & after a year or
two of bloodshed, so will Jinnah's & Pandit Nehru's.
The sun has set on this corner of our Empire & I, as an
Englishman, am deeply sorry

Incidentally, I have just had a shower, & as usual in the
hot weather, have not dried myself, but am sitting with a
towel wrapped round me. From the window I can see
into the jail compound where a game of football is in

progress. The familiar thud as brown bare foot meets
leather makes me itch to have a go, but I can't manage
football in this country. I often long for a game, & hope
I am not too old to play when I get back to Ormesby.

Today received your letter of Mar. 21st, telling of
slightly better weather, but of floods in South of England
& Midlands. In reply to your questions, Mrs. Howell is
sedate but not retiring. She can hold her own in any
company, although she always looks frail & dresses like a
bag of hammers. She does dance a little. Bob's brother
Albert is stationed in Iraq. Had a letter from him this
week telling of sand, heat & plagues of locust. I haven't
heard from Maurice Jamieson since his reply to my invitation to a dance.

Today was declared a General Strike day by the Bengal
Trades Union Council, but was postponed until next
week on account of the riots. Labour is as restless as
ever after the Gramophone Company's strike at Dum
Dum, where the men got all they asked for. Now the
Aluminium Company workers are on strike here, so
Jessop's should be next.

Last Monday evening we had a return Snooker &
Billiard match with Cossipore Club at Jessops' Club.
Being Billiard member on the Committee, I was
ex-officio captain. Alice Birchenough & Joan Farren
kindly arranged for food (snacks & sandwiches) & I had
fixed up with the Committee for free drinks for the visitors.

Being captain & sort of responsible for the evening, I
was well in the limelight: Freddy this, Freddy that, who's
playing next, skipper? Consequently, when my turn came
to play I felt very confident, & everyone expected a
marvellous game. Anyway, I played like a novice & felt
like kicking myself; but all this is part of one's education,

one cannot always win. Incidentally, we were beaten on the whole night by only nine points & I've promised the lads that next match they will have a non-playing captain, but they all insist that I play.

Last Sunday's golf match was a huge success. We three didn't play, we realized that the standard was very high & we didn't want to mess things up. We drifted round the course watching the play, and arrived back at the Clubhouse for drinks, & then tiffin. I didn't realize Jessop's has so many Europeans on the staff, mostly Clive Street, with a crowd of newcomers, mostly ex-officers demobbed in this country. I wished you could have seen the ladies' hats. They were absolutely wizard, even to a mere man. Talk about Easter Parade, & Jessop's have some very attractive mem-sahibs. Most of the ladies, including the Directors' wives had their hands full after tiffin, keeping their husbands on the straight and narrow. Messrs. Howell & Doak passed out fairly early, with Johnny High soon after. A very successful show altogether. A chap from Clive Street, Watson, won the Jardine Cup, while Dum Dum's Jock Ewing won the wooden spoon as the worst player of the day.

Well, Mam, keep the flag flying, even if you do get up to your neck in flood water. Best wishes to all at home & love.

Easter Sunday

Today, the last of the Easter break, we have had three days, Friday, Saturday & Sunday. Actually we were sched-

uled to work as usual right through, so I arranged for
cranes, machines, etc. & supervision in my department on
Thursday morning. After a union meeting at tiffin time,
the workers decided not to come in at all, & nothing we
foremen did or said changed that decision. This proves
how difficult it has become to handle & control labour
these days, due to all the unrest & uncertainty, high cost
of living, riots & strikes, etc.

With the works absolutely jammed up with orders,
we just can't get any output or get anything moving.
Absenteeism is about 40% because of transport strikes,
trains not running to schedule & Hindus & Muslims still
killing each other off all over India. Bomb throwing &
acid throwing seem to be the main sports in Calcutta
recently, although additional troops, police & curfews
have restricted the fighting lately. The only snag as far as
we are concerned is not being able to get into Calcutta.
We are tied up in Dum Dum, & short of decent food,
especially bread & beer. Beer is unobtainable & our bread
is the black, sour, Indian variety.

The renewed outbreak of killing was too much for Jack
Simpson. He went to Mr. Howell & resigned, so he has
to see the Directors now to fix up for his passage. He has
been hanging on with a view to bringing out his wife &
son; and when the recent trouble started again, he wrote
home to tell his wife it was impossible to bring her out
during the present unsettled state of the country. She
replied & said, "If I can't come out, then you have to
come home, as I am fed up with living on my own."

Life isn't very bright for us just at present, but this
month's pay includes a substantial bonus. The Indian
Government have already imposed certain restrictions on
the transfer of capital out of the country, so I am going to
increase my allowance home, just so I don't have any

money tied up in the country if we have to leave in a
hurry. Anyway Mam, stack it away in the bank for me, I
might need it within the next two years. Of course you
can use any of it that you need. By the way, I don't
remember any mention of the last two months' cheques
from you. Let me know if any are missing. You should get
a cheque regularly every 22nd or 23rd of each month,
since I arranged for air mail delivery.

        April 7th
   Since starting this letter I received one from you this
morning dated Mar. 28th, telling of safe arrival of March
cheque. Also this morning two Jessop's Directors visited
the works, first interviewing Jack Simpson &, after trying
to convince him, they accepted his resignation. They then
sent for me to tell me that they (the Board of Directors)
had sanctioned a bonus for all the imported staff, as well
as locally engaged people. I personally receive Rupees
1000/-, about £75, very encouraging. Also after a revision
of the Provident Fund, every month now, 15% of my basic
salary is salted away, instead of the previous 10% This is a
definite advantage by helping us to save (I put 7½% & the
Company doubles the amount to make 15%), while the
whole is tax free, I mean no Income tax to pay on the total
invested. Then of course, my three years are complete, so
I get another annual raise of Rs 25/- per month.
   These additions to salary etc., prove that the Company
realizes how difficult things are becoming for Europeans,
& is trying to make up by giving us more money. I had a
good laugh whilst with the Directors, Mr. Irving & Mr.
Sitwell, after they had impressed me with the need for
keeping the news under my hat. They said, "This special
bonus is for white faces only," meaning imported hands,
& not Indians & Anglo-Indians. I replied, (I had been out

in the sun all morning), "In that case, I don't qualify."
Sitwell & Irving laughed & said, "Okay, we will alter that
statement to, people with white faces, & people with
black faces but a Yorkshire accent."

We have had freak weather around Calcutta lately,
absolutely intense heat (Sunday was 104° in the shade,
about 120° in the sun), & today, although the mercury
was about 101° in the shade, the humidity was around
97% just about the limit a human being can stand. This
weather is due to hot winds blowing down from the
United Provinces, which ordinarily never reach Bengal.

Last Thursday Jessops' Billiard & Snooker team visited
the Aluminium Co.'s Fairy Hall Club for a match with the
Indian Air Survey, Bob Embleton's team. After a little
trouble getting into the Aluminium Company grounds
because of the Muslim Strike Pickets, (the Aluminium
Co. are still on strike), we arrived at the Club a little late,
but finished off all the games, Jessops' team winning
easily. This week we are arranging a return match at our
Club. Alice Birchenough & Joan Farren are fixing up the
food again for the evening. Incidentally, I take my hat off
to Joan Farren, this heat must be hellish for her. Last
Wednesday we three had dinner at the Farrens'. It was
another really hot night, & apart from the ordinary large
house fans, Joan carries around a small table tan which
she plugs into the wall wherever she goes. She says that
we three should be Godfathers by the end of this month.

We have been doing a lot of swimming lately, after
work & through the holidays. The pool is always packed
with people.

That's about all the news for the present. Give my good
wishes to all the gang, & those at home.

April 14th

Tonight being the first night we have stayed at home for
about two weeks, I am getting down to some long
delayed letter writing. Although we haven't been into
town since the Jardine Cup Golf Match, we have plenty
to do in Dum Dum. I say 'plenty to do,' but the weather
remains so hot that all we do is swim, after work during
the week, Saturday afternoons & Sundays & odd nights
up till midnight. By courtesy of the R.A.F. we have secured
a case of beer, which helps to replace (very pleasantly)
what we lose in perspiration through the day.

April 18th

You can see I didn't get much letter writing done on
the 14th. The lads dragged me off to the Club just when
I was all set, & they being in the majority (Bob & Jack),
I had to go.

Last night we played another Billiard & Snooker
Match at the Cossipore Club. After a terrifically hot day,
I had had a shower & shave after tea, & then found that I
had no clean shirts & pants to wear during the evening.
My Hindu bearer has gone on a month's leave because his
wife is ill, & Jack's bearer (a Mohommedan), with the
help of another young Mohommedan boy, is looking
after the three of us. The 'dhobi' had promised to bring
the week's washing round at 5pm, but he didn't turn up,
so I had no clean clothes. Also, the 'dhobi' being a Hindu
lives in a Hindu quarter in the bazaar, & our Muslim
bearer was scared to go into that district.

Anyway, Bob & Jack got ready & set off for the Jessops'

Club, & I grabbed hold of the Muslim bearer & told him, "Communal riots or not, I have to have a pair of clean pants, & you will have to go round to the dhobi's for them or I will start a communal riot myself."

Eventually the bearer set off, more scared of me than of a couple of thousand Hindus, & brought back my pants. I dressed quickly & started off for the Club with a clear sky overhead & in really oppressive heat. Before I was half way, the sky was black & I was mixed up in a Nor'wester cyclone, buffetted by the gale, soaked in rain & blinded with swirling dust. Reaching the Club, I found the rest of the team waiting, & also Joan Farren & Alice Birchenough.

As all the Jessop's transport was being repaired, I had arranged for a lorry to come for us from Cossipore. The lorry arrived at 8pm in pouring rain, an Indian driver & a young Lieut. & two soldiers of the Green Howards as escort. We all piled in & set off, doing about sixty miles an hour all the way, in darkness & through the rain. It was a covered lorry, but the hood was little advantage, as the front end was open & the rain drove in. Joan Farren sat on a chair in the middle & enjoyed every minute of the ride, saying it was the first time she had been cool for months. As I sat looking at the dripping trees flashing past, I was reminded of a similar ride in a lorry from Swindon to Coleshill, when I went on a demolition course in 1943 when in the Cross Keys Fusiliers.

The billiard tournament proved to be of secondary interest when we found that Fuller, a new foreman of Jessops & member of the team, could play the piano. Fuller is an Anglo-Burmese &, like Jones, my new fore-man, went back to Burma after the war, but couldn't stick it & so returned again to India. He played the piano all night in the bar; we cleared all the tables out & sang, danced & played the fool.

The Green Howards Lieutenant came from Heckmond-wyke near Leeds, so after I told him Bob came from Middlesbrough, Jack came from Rotherham, & Arthur Dwyer came from Halifax, we sang "Ilkley Moor B'aht T'At,"[46] all agreeing it is a lousy song, but the only York-shire song we knew. Just then a loud Highland Scots voice proclaimed that Yorkshire was the first Scottish Colony, but when we found the owner of the voice was about nine feet tall, we pardoned him for such a rash remark.

Later in the evening Jock Farren & Birchenough set off two fire extinguishers with the usual Dum Dum careless abandon, but we prevented them from setting fire to Cossipore Club. A very successful evening altogether, & we have a standing invitation to go there whenever we wish.

Since last night the weather has been hot, humid, showery, & tonight there is a lot of thunder & lightning, but it is slightly cooler.

Wednesday night we three went to dinner to the Kelmans'. Kelman is an Anglo-German-Indian, tall, thin, works at the Gramophone Company. He is a keen & excellent photographer, & an expert radio & recording engineer. He kept us entertained with music, & film shows from his own projector during the evening.

Sat. April 19th afternoon

Have just returned from a Lodge meeting. We usually hold our meetings during the evening through the week, but curfews & trouble in Calcutta made it necessary to have the meeting this afternoon. Our Lodge is situated in an old haunted house type of building, with dungeons, turrets, winding stairways & crumbling masonry. The building stands off the main road, overlooking a tank (lake to you) with Indian huts all around. The local

Indians call the building "Jadhu Shar," the house of magic or witchcraft.

As Bob & I passed along the path by the lake on the way in, I saw what I have not seen before in three years in India. The whole Indian community lined the banks of the lake cheering & chattering, while in the water, just over their waists, were a couple of hundred young Indians whacking the water with long bamboos, continually. The whole thing seemed senseless to me, as I didn't see anyone catch any fish. However, when the meeting ended & as we walked back, the crowd still lined the lake edge, but no one was in the water. Everyone was picking up fish, half stunned, flopping about at the water's edge, & in ten minutes we saw about 200 fish, all about two to two and a half pounds in weight, just lifted out of the lake as easy as that. So now you know how to catch fish.

Remember me to everyone at Ormesby, & best wishes to all at home.

June 2nd

I see from your last letter that you safely received the cheque for £37-7-5d, but there is no need for sending a wire. Obviously you are not getting all my mail, because I mentioned previously in three letters that I was going to transfer some of my capital to England before the Indian Govt. stopped me. I haven't heard from Ernie for quite a long time, although I had a brief air letter from Ethel. It is hard luck if mail goes astray, especially now, when we can't get air letters (6 annas) & have to write big six page efforts.

The Viceroy is back in India with the solution to all the

problems of Hindustan & Pakistan. So certain are we, the
Europeans, of trouble on the day of the announcement,
now put back to June 5th, that we have all got in supplies
of tinned stuff in case a first class war starts. Calcutta is
absolutely swarming with British & Gurkha soldiers,
Pathan, Punjabi & Bengali police placed in strategic
positions all over the city by Premier Suhrawardy &
Governor Burrows, to crush immediately any attempt at
rioting. Even with all these precautions there were the
usual daily killings & burning of houses yesterday. One of
my Hindustani rivetters was stabbed to death during
Sunday night in Calcutta; I allowed ten of his pals to leave
work early this morning to carry his body down to the
ghats for burning. The ten rivetters would probably set
fire to a couple of Mohommedan houses on the way back,
just for fun.

Pakistan is already set up & it is definite that the
Muslims will get a separate state. Personally I am glad to
see Pakistan, most of the Europeans prefer Muslims to
Hindus.

The current Muslim doggerel is:

Kân mên biri (Cigarette behind your ear)
(ear) (in) (cigarette)
Moue mên pân (Betel-nut in your mouth)
(mouth) (in) (betel nut)
Lar-ke lengê (After fighting will take)
(fighting from) (will take)
Pakistan (Pakistan)

The Congress Indians have another saying: Muslims
want Pakistan, Hindus want Hindusthan, we will all get
Kabristan. Kabr is Urdu for grave, Kabristan being a
humorous word for cemetery. Meanwhile the country
goes from bad to worse, with a shortage of food, shortage
of cloth, & most of all, a shortage of common sense.

The Birchenoughs' & Farrens' party was a huge success
on Sat. evening. The arrangement was grand, being a very
hot sticky night, we all came attired in short sleeved shirts
open at the neck & white slacks. The lawn was flood-lit,
with a large tarpaulin sheet stretched out for dancing. A
bar was rigged up in the summerhouse, & the radiogram
on the verandah. The high spot of the evening was when I
put the "Nutcracker Suite" on the radiogram, & Jock
Farren in tights & Arthur Dwyer in a ballet skirt, danced a
wonderful ballet on the lawn. Bill Howell fell over laughing & sat in the rum punch bowl. The only casualties
were: three of the Air Survey chaps who drove their car
into the pond at the end of the compound (they only got
wet); & Jock Farren, who has the most wonderful pair of
black eyes. While turning a somersault over three chairs
stood in a line, he bumped his face with his knees. I
almost forgot, Birch was barman, & he put his arm into
the table fan while leading the singing at the bar. Alex
Smith was there, too. It was the first time I'd seen him in
three months.

Incidentally, while I am writing there is a terrific Nor'
wester storm raging, a very welcome change from the
heat of today. By the sound of the gale & the rain, the
monsoons must have started two weeks too early.

Last week we went to dinner to the Fairy Hall Club
with the Westmorelands. I ate about six whole ducks
myself. "Westy" is the manager of the Aluminium
Company at Dum Dum & his men are still on strike.
Nine weeks now, with no hope of a settlement so far. So
Westy is having a long holiday on full pay.

When Mrs. Ewing left Bombay she flew to Calcutta,
sending all her luggage by rail. Of course, it was all stolen,
as usual in India. She is in a mess now because she has
no clothes, & their son, who should be in school in

Darjeeling, has lost all his warm clothing too, so he has to stay in Dum Dum at present. Fortunately the luggage was insured, so they won't lose financially.

The other night, just as I had started a letter, a note came round from Kelman, asking if we would like to go to the pictures &, if so, to turn up at his bungalow by 7:30 pm. As I haven't seen a film since New Year, I jumped at the offer. So Bob & I set off to the Kelmans' wondering how we were going to get into Calcutta through the curfews.

Arriving at the bungalow, we were introduced to a youngish Englishman named Beard, manager of the Kodak Company in Calcutta. Mr. & Mrs. Kelman, Bob & I climbed into Beard's car (the very latest model Chrysler just out from home) & set off, not towards Calcutta, but straight into the heart of the jungle. After half an hour's ride among thick vegetation on a rough road, we turned in at a very impressive gateway & drove through a magnificent compound, pulling up at the porch of large, beautiful house. It had been built by a cracked millionaire & was taken over by Beard. I was really surprised to find such a building, with every modern device, in such a lonely & jungli spot. Beard showed us his glasshouse, packed with orchids, his large tiled swimming pool, packed with snakes, & his cocktail cabinet, packed with everything from Drambuie to beer. While sampling the beer, we were introduced to his black Himalayan bear cub, a friendly little so & so who tried to chew off my calf muscles. This type Beard had everything: radio, radiogram, shortwave receiver & transmitter, & a first class talkie film unit.

We sat back under the fan, toying with Scotch whisky, while we saw the film "State Fair," & afterwards "Rhapsody in Blue." Finishing up with a sing-song,

which Beard thoroughly enjoyed, we came back home in
his car at about two am.

Still another peculiar & interesting type, very different,
with everything money can buy. A bachelor, living miles
from anywhere, who really got a kick out a singing a few
old songs horribly out of tune.

The results of Mountbatten's efforts have just been
announced. He gave a speech on the radio, followed by
Pandit Jawaharlal Nehru, Mohammed Ali Jinnah, &
Sardar Baldev Singh. To my way of thinking, England still
leads the world in the diplomatic field. What a marvellous
solution to the Indian problem, someone in the British
Government has got brains. Think it over, Mam: the
Indians shout for freedom; the British say, okay, go
ahead; the Indians go ahead & start to wipe each other
out; the situation becomes a mess; the British say, "Get
organized, we are leaving in 1948"; the situation becomes
more confused, even after trying like hell they can't stop
the riots; now the British say, "You can't get organized, so
we are going to sort it out: two Dominions, & stop the
scrapping." Anyway, we haven't lost India yet.

Best of luck to all.

June 17th

The monsoons have commenced with all the usual trimmings, a heavy thunderstorm starting yesterday, lasting
throughout the night with the end of the thunder at tiffin
time today, but still raining. Actually, during the recent
two weeks we have had several false starts to the monsoon

with intermittent days of terrific heat & humidity.

Last Thursday, the King Emperor's birthday & a holiday for us, was the hottest day this year. Fortunately, being a holiday, we could swim all day, although several of the Dum Dum crowd, Bill Howell, Birchenough, etc. went on a binge in the Clubhouse & did some heavy drinking while they played snooker. I was amused at Birch when, at 2:30 pm, under a new rule of the committee, the bar closed until the evening. Birch came weaving out of the Club & set off home, but just as he passed through the main gates he had a parting shot at the committee for closing the bar. He said, "King George would be ruddy-well annoyed if he knew that Jessop's Club had stopped serving drinks on his birthday, at tiffin time."

Probably the last King of England's birthday which will be celebrated in this country, & incidentally, all cinemas have discontinued playing the National Anthem at the end of performances.

My new foreman, Jones, who came from Burma, has packed in & leaves for England & Huddersfield in August. All my assistants are now Indians, although Howell told me that Jessops are trying to bring out two more British foremen.

Last week in my capacity as Billiards member of the Club, I ordered the works' car & went into Calcutta to purchase billiard cues & carpets. The name of the firm I called at was John Roberts (Madras). *The* John Roberts was a professional in England, came out East & started the firm; his grandson, John Roberts, is now in charge & I met him personally, & his wife. After all the work the family have put into the business, they are now selling out & Mrs. Roberts is leaving this month for Ireland, her home. Her husband probably has some Eurasian blood in his veins, but his father was a Lancashire man. As soon as I had introduced myself he said, "How good to hear a good North Country accent," & I thought I had lost all trace of it now, after three years in India.

Re. Mountbatten & India, I think the British Government have done some fine work in putting him in charge. He has done more in one month than Nehru & Company have done in a year towards settling India's problems. Definitely, Pakistan & Hindustan is a very poor solution, but under the circumstances, the only possible way to ensure peace in India.

Personally, I think that the Indian Leaders are surprised, themselves, at the complexity of the problems confronting them, the hate & distrust which all the different Jats (types) feel for each other. In plain words, they have bitten off more than they can chew & after Nehru's speech when he said, "We will not accept anything but a united India, & we want nothing whatever to do with the British Empire," & Jinnah, who said, "Nothing but complete Independence for Muslims, with a Pakistan including Bengal, Punjab & Assam *unpartitioned*," now they both agree to Hindustan & Pakistan within the British Empire as Dominions, & have also submitted to division of Bengal & Punjab. Naturally this partition of states will cause trouble, but if India is still within the Empire, our troops can remain & stop any riots immediately.

Incidentally, we expected trouble on the 5th of June, but Calcutta passed a quiet day, while rioting in town has almost stopped.

Of course the solution to the Indian problem is that there is no solution. They will never agree. Just imagine 273 different languages, with over 2000 dialects, castes, jats, religions, races, creeds.

The other night I was having a nap just before going
out to dinner. The bearer awoke me & said I had a visitor.
Going into the dining room, I was surprised to find
Rashu Mukherjhee, the Bengali Brahmin who used to
visit us when we lived with Alex Smith in the compound.
I hadn't seen him for twelve months. Same old Rashu,
clad in an old shirt & dhoti which must have cost him
about ten rupees, his old car downstairs. Yet wrapped
round his waist in that same old dhoti, he carries a couple
of lakhs of rupees, more than I could save if I lived to be a
thousand. His village, Badhu, mostly Muslim, is to be in
Pakistan & Rashu takes a dim view of the arrangement.
He says he will fight until Badhu is Hindustan.

His English is about as good as my Bengali, so we lace
the conversation with Hindi & Urdu, & get along without noticing the difference. Rashu brought us some
mangoes, ee-speshul for us, so we would not forget
Rashu. He spoke the truth, the mangoes were wizard.
A good mango eaten at the correct time is the most delicious fruit in the world.

Last Saturday, still not fixed up with billiards carpets,
I got permission to enter Dum Dum Jail. Our Planning
Office foreman is a Bengali named Bose, & his uncle,
named Dutta, is the superintendent of the Jail, so he
accompanied me. The convicts do a lot of weaving, rope-
making & coir work,[47] so I wanted to see if they could
make me some mats for the Club. So far, Dum Dum Jail
is the only Indian-run concern I have yet seen, which is
efficient, clean & well organized. The superintendent,
Dutta, is a really remarkable man, well liked, go-ahead,
etc. (although I noticed he sucks his teeth, chews pan
(betel nut), scratches himself while he talks, in typical
Bengali style).

I hope you are interested in these ramblings, but nothing of exceptional interest happens in Dum Dum.

Enclosed snaps are: No. 1, some of the Structural foremen. left to right: Miguel de Rosario Gaston da Alva, a
Bangalore Indian Christian whose ancestors were
converted by the early Portuguese settlers; Walter Brooks,
Anglo-Indian Preparing Dept. foreman; Fred Brennan,
domiciled Irishman, Press Shop foreman (I visited his
kids at school in Darjeeling); Smith, a Scot with some
Indian blood, who got beaten up by some goondahs who
broke into his Calcutta house (he got scared & resigned &
is waiting for his passage); Sarendra Nath Chandra
Dutta, a Bengali who took over Jack Simpson's job. By
the way, we had a letter from "Simmy"[48] today, back in
Rotherham after a lousy trip in a dormitory crammed
with Armenians & Indians. He is having a holiday, but
has written for a foreman's job in Manchester.

No. 2 snap: a view of the Royal Calcutta Golf
Clubhouse from the first hole. This is where we ran the
Jessops' golf competition, a wonderful building inside.

No. 3, left to right: Arthur Dwyer driving off (that's
what he thinks, he will probably miss the ball); Parkinson
from Clive St. office; & Jock Farren, who should be a
father when you get this letter.

Seeing in your last letter that Woodhead had left
Cargo Fleet & Alf Perry[49] was once more in command,
I mentioned it to Howell, but he hadn't heard anything.
He evidently doesn't correspond with his wife's people.
His daughter Joan (17 years old) has just heard that she
has passed her Junior Cambridge & Matric. Exams, so
she is finished with schooling & joins sister Sheila in the
ranks of the idle rich.

Hope you all keep fit & interested. I do, & so far have
not found any cause to run away from India. Best wishes
to you-all, & Love.

July 7th

Have received two letters from you, telling of Dad's holiday & proposed trips to Harrowgate, Redcar, Lake
District, etc.; I was surprised to read that you weren't
going away anywhere for the full fortnight. Surely you
could find a cottage up in the dales or stay with one of our
many relatives scattered around in England. Anyway,
what about one of those fascinating Polytechnic tours to
Switzerland or Italy; fly there & back & quite cheap too.
Is the regular holiday in England now two weeks with
pay, or is yours a special case?

My holiday is not far distant, & as usual I am
confronted with the complex problem of deciding where
to go: Darjeeling again, Gopalpur again, Bombay, a
shooting trip in Assam, a three weeks journey up the
Brahmaputra by river-steamer to Dibrugash in Assam, or
to Rangoon by 'plane'? Anyway, it may be difficult for
travelling. We may even require passports to get from
Dum Dumistan to Hindusthan or Pakistan, or find that
railways are on strike or something.

Several of the gang in Dum Dum, myself included,
have received cards from Jack Simpson in Scarborough,
where he is on holiday. He says he is having a wizard time,
although the weather is damned cold.

The other night, after attending a committee meeting
of Jessop's Club, I came home &, being on my own,
tuned in the radio for some music. Getting a programme
from Singapore, I sat back & listened to an orchestra
playing the Destiny Waltz, & realized that I would give a
thousand chips to be able to go to an Ormesby Saturday

night dance (if they still run them).

Our Club has been pretty lively lately. On Thursday I fixed up a billiard & snooker tournament with the Air Survey team, with swimming & dancing on the verandah. On Saturday evening, John Beard, the manager of Kodak Company in Calcutta, brought along his film show. We all sat on the verandah with a screen rigged up on the tennis court. He showed "Rhapsody in Blue" first, & the audience was so enthusiastic that he put on as an encore "This is the Army." This film I had already seen at the Warner Theatre, Leicester Square in London under very different surroundings.

While we were watching the show, Birchenough, Howell & Doak, not being very interested in films, decided to play snooker. So, we blacked out the windows & they remained in the Clubhouse.

The show lasted from 8pm to 1am & when we re-entered the Club we found that Birch, Howell & Co. had been doing some steady drinking with the bar to themselves. Their respective mem-sahibs eyed the battlefield with strong disapproval & soon hustled their protesting husbands into the car & off home, to bed.

Bill Howell really has a rough time with his wife & two daughters. They keep him in line, & there is nothing old Bill likes better than a drink & a game of snooker. The other night he came into the Club alone for one game, having promised Doris he would be back home by 8pm. At midnight he was sitting next to me enjoying himself immensely, when the doorway was suddenly filled with Mrs. Howell (with a glint in her eye) & her two six foot daughters, looking very tough. Bill said, "Oh hell, here comes the enemy, give your wrong names, here's a copper." Then, his daughters taking position at either side of him, Mrs. Howell leading the procession, they

marched him off to bed. We often get a laugh at Uncle
Bill.

Yesterday, Sunday, we went to Chandernagore, a
French colony or possession. Young Joan Devereaux, the
daughter of one of Jessops' Mechanical Works foremen,
was going back to school, or rather, convent, & we
decided to go too, never having been to Chandernagore
before. Bob, myself, Arthur Dwyer, Mrs. Devereaux, &
her son & daughter, Jock & Joan, made up the party,
setting off in the station wagon at 10am.

The weather was fine & hot, & the drive was very pleasant to Bally, among the jute mills on the banks of the
Hooghly River. Here we left the car & caught a train to
Chandernagore, about fifteen miles up the river. During
the one hour's journey it started to rain, pouring down
onto the already flooded paddy fields, & drumming onto
the bamboo, box-like structures (about 100 feet x 100 feet
x 5 feet high) where the natives grow the pan leaf, or betel
nut, as you know it.

Leaving the train at Chandernagore station, Bob & the
Devereauxs got into a bund gharry, a closed horse-drawn
cab. Arthur & I got into a ricksha & got thoroughly
soaked during the ride to the convent. We sat in the reception room drying out, & one of the French nuns came to
talk to us. I wasn't very impressed with the convent as an
institution of learning. Too many statues, religious paint-
ings, nuns in long white robes & a church-like atmosphere. Anyway, we said goodbye to young Joan (who
seemed quite at home), & walked along the riverside (the
rain had ceased). In front of the huge Gothic Church (I
think early French Colonial buildings were Gothic) was a
huge plinth with a bust of Monsieur Le Governeur
Dupliex, who was the Governor of all French Indian
possessions in 1659. A really fine looking guy in a curled

wig; as I said "Hyah, Bud," I mentally raised my hat, to
him & the other early French, Portuguese & English
adventurers who sailed from Europe in a wooden boat
with a couple of sails, with not much idea of where they
were going, but plenty of guts, to build trade & Empires
in the far East.

Chandernagore is fairly clean, very much like other
small Indian towns except for the native gendarmes &
civic buildings with signs in French.

After tiffin in a café, we sat on the riverbank (the
Hooghly is about a mile wide here),& watched the native
boats swinging past, some sideways, some stern first,
some with lug sails & all with ten or twelve men on the
oars, which they use standing up, one step forward & one
step back, & getting some real speed out of their boats.
The tide was coming in from the sea, ninety miles away, &
with a following wind, the boats seemed to whirl past like
leaves in a rain-swept gutter.

Leaving Chandernagore at 4:30pm we were back in
Bally by 5:30pm, where we visited some jute wallah
friends of Arthur's. At 8pm our car turned up, with
Rezzak the Mohemmedan driver scared to death because
we had to drive home through a curfew area. The curfew
is for the inhabitants, but through traffic is allowed on the
main road. We were stopped twice by Indian troops in tin
hats, with rifles with fixed bayonets, & our car was thoroughly searched. There has been an increase in rioting in
Calcutta recently, & many goondahs are travelling
around, armed to the teeth, in stolen cars.

Today we had a few showers, but so far the monsoons
have been very in-active & Bombay has the driest June for
over 100 years.

You should be getting some fine weather now, with a
hot sun of about 65° at midday. If I should get into a

temperature of less than 80° I would freeze.

The next time you write, Mam, let me know what wages Dad, Arthur & Violet are getting, just so I can get a rough idea of salaries & cost of living at home. My best wishes to you all.

July 14th

A sunny evening, but with a dark horizon & a wind blowing the rain clouds this way; in fact, typical monsoon weather.

I am staying in the bungalow to give my face a rest from shaving, my beard grows like wildfire now & is as tough as barbed wire.

Today received your short letter telling of your attendance at the wedding of Harry Wood & Mary. I think I remember Harry Wood, but Mary I don't know, & Florrie Daggett[50] was a school kid when I left home, but much water has passed under the bridge since then.

The situation in India is deteriorating rapidly, with rioting & killing once more spreading. Last week was pretty gruesome in Calcutta, none of the foremen or men residing in town were able to get into work. The rioting goondahs are becoming more civilized these days; by more civilized, I mean that instead of using knives & soda water bottles, they now ride in jeeps, armed with automatic weapons, sten guns, grenades & bombs. Almost everyday last week bombs were thrown into crowded trams (those that were running). This week practically the whole of Calcutta is under curfew, all owners of military

jeeps & vehicles are now under strict supervision, & the
streets are deserted after 7pm.

Shortage & non-supply of material is crippling all
industry, Jessop's being in the 'same boat', having thousands of orders on hand, but not being able to get on with
the job for a thousand reasons, strikes in smaller supplying firms, restrictions on railway freight & dispatching,
with a lot of electric motors, machinery & fittings imported from U.K. & U.S.A. held up at the docks.

I almost forgot, Jessops are suffering from a shortage
of supervisory staff & common or garden foremen.

Local news of interest to you is that Joan & Jock Farren
now have a healthy son, Ian, who was born in Riordan
Nursing Home, Calcutta, nine days ago. Joan & Ian are
coming back to Dum Dum tomorrow.

Poor old Arthur Dwyer has got dysentery & is getting
the usual injections of emetine. Alex Smith was staying
with his daughter (Mrs. Birchenough) this weekend, &
he & I had a laugh (cruel of us) over the agony that his old
bathroom had seen. When we four were living together,
(Bob & I, Alex & Jack Simpson), Bob & I had one bathroom & Alex & Jack the other. When Jack got his dose of
dysentery, he could always be found in the bathroom,
morning, noon & night, & Alex had to come over to our
side. Then of course before that Pete Page & Bob were
always fighting to get in, & now Arthur Dwyer (lodging
with the Birchenoughs) has just spent four days there.
Alex Smith suggests that they have a radio installed, ready
for the next victim (he has my sympathies, even with a
radio).

I read the account of General Slim's retreats &
advances against the Japs in Burma, & the one thing I
respected the British soldier for during those campaigns,
was that he fought whilst suffering from dysentery. One

of General Slim's orders of the day was, "Never mind your pants, keep marching & don't drop out in the jungle or you get left behind to certain death." I suppose very few people in England really understand what that means.

Last Saturday night John Beard brought his film show to the Club once more, & showed the film "Weekend at the Waldorf," which I had already seen but thoroughly enjoyed; in my opinion this is one of the most entertaining American films produced for a long time. There was quite a large audience on the Club verandah, most of whom had not been able to get into town to a cinema for two or three months.

Tomorrow evening, Bob & I are going round to the Doaks' for dinner, with some chess after with Mr. Doak. Quite a long time since I played chess, but I still remember what old Lowell taught me about the game when I used to sneak out of the village hall dance on a Saturday & into the Lowells' house. That was before I learnt to dance, & was learning to play chess with old Lowell.

There must be some pretty dark-skinned immigrants coming into England just at present. The Anglo-Indian population of India are leaving in thousands for "home", as they call England. One of the Mechanical Works foremen, an Anglo-Indian named Fuller, is sending his wife & two girls "home" next month. They are going to Shipley & I was explaining to them last Saturday night how cold it is on Ilkla' Moor B'aht T'aht. One of the girls is very fair & the other is very dark but very beautiful; I'll bet she isn't a wallflower at Bradford dances.

I don't know whether you remember me mentioning a domiciled European named Carr, who was sent to England by his father before the war for training in the aircraft business. Anyway, this guy Carr married a North

Ormesby girl from Telford Street. He came back to India
& worked for Dalmia Jain Airways at Dum Dum, & his
wife also came out with their small daughter. They lived
in Digla Road behind the Structrual Works. I never
met the North Ormesby girl, she has been staying in
Jubbulpore for about a year, but last week, in the Club,
the small girl (about 7 or 8 years old) came up to me &
said, "Do you know my uncle Dick, Dick Kershaw?"
Well, I know him well, so does Dad. Dick is older than me
& works (or worked) in the boiler shop as a plater with
me. Small world & all that.

I see in today's paper that the Indian Government have
further reduced the amount that can be sent out of the
country monthly, from £250 per month to £100 per
mensem. It doesn't affect me yet, actually, but it will; in
the meantime I shall continue sending my £37 odd home
to you.

Incidentally, today I received a letter from my bank,
telling me that my account had been debited 10 chips for
permitting me to lend them money. The only 'ruddy'
bank I have heard of which *charges* one for investing one's
money.

Since I started this letter the rain has started, & Bob is
in the next room with the radio going, a programme from
either Saigon or Indonesia, a cinema organ playing some
old tunes. Bob says it sounds like the Elite & I say it
sounds like the Gaumont.[51] By the way, Bob is rapidly
losing his hair & now has a completely bald patch on the
top. He could pass easily for 35.

He has taken on the secretaryship of our Club. Howell
is chairman, I am in charge of sports & competitions. In
fact, Bill Howell spends more time messing about for the
Club than he spends in his job at work. I haven't seen him
round the shops for days, which is unusual for him.

Well Mam, great changes are still taking place in India & anything can happen in the next three or four months, so don't be surprised if I write to you from New Zealand or South Africa one day. I still keep my eyes open for a chance. All the British Dominions are asking for immigrants, & personally I think there is more opportunity abroad than in England. Things still sound very difficult for you back there, it seems to be all wrong for us to be borrowing American money to exist. Keep fit & enjoy yourself. My best wishes to you all.

July 28th

Dear Violet,

Thanks a lot for your letter, (even if it was written in a one-finger flowing backhand). Incidentally, Mam takes a dim view of typed correspondence, apart from business letters; she says it is difficult to judge character by studying a letter composed by a stenographer on a busman's holiday; and I think her reasoning is correct.

Wasn't it Browning who used to knock off thousands of sweetie pie letters to somebody's wife? I suppose the literary value of the same 'billets deux' would have been much reduced if he had typed them. However if you attempt to read my character from this effort, you will probably come to the conclusion that I need a new pen, new ink & a new "Webster's."

These days I find it increasingly difficult to write; not that my life is so uninteresting, but the 'news' value of my scribblings is not very high to any reader in England. After all, the average person in U.K. expects to get "the India problem in a nutshell," or "A quick solution to the India puzzle" from me everytime I write, & I doubt if Mountbatten, Jinnah & Nehru could oblige with such a letter.

The policy of the British Government is clear, they wish to hand over the country to the Indians, absolutely, but still want to keep a friendly India within the Commonwealth as a market for British goods; & personally I think this is the right attitude, & Mountbatten has done a wonderful job in setting up two Dominions. Meanwhile, during the transitional period, the country is in one hell of a mess, politically, economically & financially, with riots, strikes, rationing, shortages, partitioning, inflation, racial intolerance, in fact, all the evils of the post war world, with the worst black market & system of bribery of any country. We, as Europeans, all hope that we will be living in Pakistan. We would have a much better time with the Muslims than with the Hindus (the lesser of two evils).

In any case, I think that my days are numbered in India. I've seen it all, & would like to find me a job in some country where the population is European & the weather sub-tropical (it seems that New Zealand is indicated). Even the most optimistic Europeans realize that they will not be very welcome in a free (?) India; hence the mad rush for shipping & passports, especially among the Anglo-Indians or Eurasians. England must be full of them by this time with lots more to come. Incidentally, you probably wouldn't recognize an Anglo-Saxophone if you saw one, Anglo-Indian being an ambiguous term covering everything from Christian Madrassis with names like D'Souzo, D'Rosario, D'Alva (converts of the early Portuguese settlers) to Domiciled Europeans. As a matter of fact, true Britishers are now a rarity in a country which becomes more foreign every day; with new restrictions being introduced in a direct attempt to drive us out.

The weather remains like the political situation, unsettled, moody & stormy, & all wet; we are now in the middle of the Southerly monsoons. India being geographically like a huge saucer with the Himalayas & the sea as the rim, the monsoons commence by belts of low pressure drifting down from the north & then coming back over & drifting round & round the saucer for three months from mid-July.

I shall probably take my leave after the rains at the end of September, & have been 'toying' with the idea of going to Rangoon, providing I can find someone who has been before & knows the ropes; this used to be a popular holiday for Calcutta sahibs pre-war.

Your life seems to be made up of classes, study & very little real leisure. Don't you ever "beat it up" & get away from all this education? By the way, the experts say that every person has a distinct flair for some subject, some field in which he or she is above average. Well, I often wondered what my particular bent was, being a structural engineer more by force of circumstance than by inclination; & eventually I have found that languages seems to be the subject in which I excel. I can even think in Hindi & converse in the slang with all the catch phrases & sayings of the real dialect which cannot be found in any book. Also I can speak Bengali passably which is a tongue of an entirely different source to Hindi or Urdu. I feel rather proud of this achievement actually, because not one sahib in a thousand ever learns Bengali, while pronunciation is very difficult.

I can't remember seeing any books by the authors

whose names you quoted in your letter, probably because
I haven't been into a bookstall for months, not being able
to visit Calcutta these days. However, I would recom-
mend you to join the "Book-of-the-Month Club," 385
Madison Avenue, New York 17, N.Y., this organization
being the source of supply of most of my reading matter.
The only snag is that you-all should cut down your overseas spending, especially in U.S.A. I suppose it is not very
patriotic to purchase American publications.

Talking (or writing) of books reminds me that I have a
sneaking idea to write a book myself. You see, we, the
British population of Dum Dum, are living at present a
life in a sort of backwater, away from the rest of the world.
Thrown together, we have to make our own fun, &
consequently get to know each other better than neigh-
bours usually do. We live a rather peculiar existence,
everyone's character & idiosyncracies being known, &
our little colony is made up of the most diverse & interesting people one could hope to find. Anyway, you probably recognize the theme, human interest & all that. My
command of English is not up to usual literary standards,
but I might get away with it by writing in the vernacular
as Richard Llewellyn did in *None But The Lonely Heart* &
How Green Was My Valley. Actually, I am not quite certain
of the approved style of Mss. or how to draw my royalties,
otherwise I should be on the road to fame. Afterthought:
the sahibs in our backwater respect the chastity of each
others' wives, so the book probably wouldn't sell anyway.

I haven't heard from Ernie Cooper for quite a while, so
I realize that things aren't as they should be in England; I
have noted with interest the tone of Ernie's letters getting
gloomier & gloomier in the last two years; he is very
disappointed in the Labour Govt. Personally, as a mere
onlooker, I would say the British Public are more to

blame for the "more money, less work" policy, than is the
Labour Govt.

The enclosed snap is an absolutely authentic &
untouched photograph of myself doing about ten knots
in the deep end (note the ~~phisyque physyque phys~~ – see
how well built I am).

Best wishes to you & the family.

Love, Fred

P.S. THIS COUNTRY IS RIPE FOR COMMUNISM.

Sunday Aug. 10th

Dear Mam,

A quiet Sunday evening at home with the weather still
wet & sultry, in fact this morning while I was round at the
Club playing the usual gang at snooker, the rain came
down in the proverbial 'sheets.' The last week has been a
long succession of showers & the roads have been
ankle-deep in water, with all the rain which we should
have had last month.

Consequently, with all the bad weather we have had,
our social life has been restricted & so I haven't a lot of
news to write about. We haven't even been swimming
lately. However, just to give you some idea of what we do
with ourselves these days I shall record our last week's
activities.

Monday: Work from 8am & a busy morning for me with

I.S.D. inspectors. Incidentally, we are so shorthanded that I am now running the Structural assembly, crane assembly, wagon assembly, & am erecting a new bay for the fabrication of Road Rollers. Since Jack Simpson & Jones left, we are having a busy time, & now all my Anglo Indian & European foremen having left, all my assistants are Bengali Hindus: Ghose, Sadhukhan, Paul, Bannerjhee, & Thakur.

After tiffin I took out the new Chevrolet station wagon from the Structural Works & drove down to the site of the Cossipore Electric Power Station. We are doing the steelwork: it will be the largest Power Station in India & will supply most of Calcutta.

I had a talk with Jenrick the Site Engineer, about a few snags on the job, & then had a walk round with him, feeling very proud to have helped in the building of so massive a structure. I saw the erectors (all Punjabis) lift a thirty ton girder into position, & then left.

The road runs through what the Indians call the "Chirya Khana," Chirya meaning bird, & Khana meaning building. Some Raja used to keep a zoo or bird house (aviary) at this spot on the corner of the Barrackpore Trunk Road & Cossipore Road. A very tough quarter, there are always killings & riots here, & my Hindu driver was scared stiff. However the roadside was lined with Gurkha soldiers & armoured cars & we passed without incident.

After work Bob & I attended the Lodge of Instruction at Dum Dum. The lodge finished up at 10:30 and after dinner we retired to bed.

Tuesday: After the usual day at work, we went straight over to the Club to a committee meeting to fix up entertainments & check accounts. When the meeting was ended at 7pm we got out the cues & had a session at

snooker, breaking up at 11pm when Mrs. Howell, Mrs.
Farren & Mrs. Birchenough turned up to see if their
husbands were coming for tea.

Wednesday: As we had an open invitation to visit the
Farrens' since last week, we had decided to go round
Wednesday. After a smooth shave & donning our long
pants (not often I wear them), we set off for the Farrens'
at 7pm & as the road passes the Club, Bob said, "We had
better run past in case anyone drags us in." Anyway,
Arthur Dwyer did call us in as we approached & after a
drink we excused ourselves & set off again at 7:30 pm. As
we entered the compound, Birch called out to us from his
verandah, which was a blaze of light (it is dark at 7
o'clock). He was sitting alone with his wife, Alice. Birch is
in disgrace because his last Club bill was 500 chips, so
Alice was keeping him indoors. They were pleased as hell
to see us, so we went in & had a drink, listened to the
radio, while Alice showed us her electric Singer sewing
machine, a really fine piece of work.

Again excusing ourselves, we finally reached the
Farrens at 9 pm. Little Ian was snoring like a pig, & I sat
on the floor with their three wire-haired terrier pups,
while Joan rustled us some grub from the ice-box. We left
at about 1 am, after talking ourselves hoarse for about
three hours.

Thursday: I had decided I was going to have a quiet night
in the bungalow writing letters, but my hopes were
rudely shattered when Bob's brother's army friend, Ken,
turned up, & then Arthur Dwyer called in. So the night
was spent in taking indoor snaps, fooling around & playing the radiogram.

Friday: Another special Lodge night with a supper afterwards in the Fairy Hall Club.

Saturday: After work, we had a Madrassi Indian chap in

for tiffin. He is a Jessops' accountant & has been checking
over the Club's books. The postman arrived at 3 pm with
a stack of mail for me, a letter from Jack Simpson saying
he misses the cigarettes, beer, impromptu parties, free &
easy life, snooker, sun, heat & swimming of Dum Dum.
He is still doing nothing & is browned off. He says he is
applying for any job from plater's helper to Works
Director without any luck. After August holidays he is
going up to his old firm in Tyneside to see if there are any
jobs going.

There were three bundles of mail from you (magazines), thanks very much. I always appreciate them &
get a good idea of world events from News Review, &
pictures of England keep me up with the times. There was
also a letter mentioning that Gracie Fields was singing at
Middlesbrough Town Hall. Coincidentally, there has just
been a Gracie Fields programme on our radio from Roch-
dale, a re-broadcast from Radio s.e.a.c. Ceylon. She still
seems to hold the audiences as she used to do & her voice
& spirits seem unimpaired with the passage of time.

I was going to finish this letter here, but think I can
manage another two pages. After reading your magazines
I had my afternoon siesta, awakening at 7 pm for a bath &
shave before going to the Club. Our entertainment for
the night consisted of two hours "Housey" on the verandah (a game which is played a lot in India in Clubs). Then
we had dancing to the radiogram. There was a large
crowd there (for Dum Dum) & I thoroughly enjoyed
myself. I like a good dance. Alex Smith was there too, as
full of fun as ever. The night was also a sort of farewell
party for Mrs. Fuller & her two daughters. They are sailing for England tomorrow. I think I mentioned it in a
previous letter that they are going to Shipley Yorks.
Anyway, that concludes my week, & you can see that we

have plenty to do without getting bored, even though we can't get into town.

This next week will be a momentous week for India. The two new Dominions take over from Aug. 15th, & the works are to be closed from that day until Aug. 18th, four days' holiday. We have had our instructions from the Bengal Chamber of Commerce, through our Head Office, that the Dominion Flag is to be hoisted alone on the 15th over the three works, & afterwards is to be flown side by side with the Union Jack. We are definitely to be in the Dominion of Hindusthan at Dum Dum, as per the decision of the boundary commission.

What will happen from the 15th onwards, no one can say, but I have an idea that there will be some real trouble in Calcutta because of the large Muslim population who object to living in Hindusthan. The City is packed with Military & police reinforcements, almost all Indian, but still the killings continue. There has been a further deterioration in the last few days, & Gandhi is now in Calcutta trying to stop the rioting.

At Lodge on Friday night the Cossipore members told us they saw a man killed under their noses. As they climbed into their station wagon just inside the main gates of the Cossipore Estate, a Muslim stabbed a passing Hindu & ran off. The Hindu ran inside the gate & then crumpled up dead. These Indians must really hate each other to stab one another in cold blood like this, & for no good reason either. Anyway, it is worthwhile for me to stay on for a while, until the rest of the world becomes more settled (& the money is good here, too). Best wishes to all the family. Jai Hind & Pakistan Zindabad.

Aug. 19th

A foreigner in a foreign land, from now on; no longer the ruling class, but still entitled to respect as a technician, as long as I remain fair and firm.

So far I have had no insubordination or lack of respect from my men; on the contrary, the last two days I have had deeper salaams than usual; and where one or two have somewhat timidly greeted me with "Jai Hind," I answered with the customary "Bande Mataram" and found they appreciated it.

The nearest approach to an insult was on the morning of the 16th, during the four day holiday. As I was walking round to the Club I passed a group of Bengalis; one of them turned to his companion & said, "Amar naukar achché," or translated, "Here is my servant." Speaking in Bengali, he naturally thought I didn't understand, so I let it pass, partly because just behind them was a party of Hindustani wardens from the Jail armed with lathis,[52] & I didn't want to start a riot while they were so excited over their "Swaraj" (Independence).

As a matter of fact, I pull Hinduism, Nehru, Gandhi, & especially Subhas Chandra Bose[53] to pieces when talking to my men, & they don't seem to mind. I think if there ever was any trouble directed against the sahibs in this country, I could rely on my fellows 100%.

Of course it has been sensible to keep out of Calcutta lately, it is rather like Chicago in the bad old days of gangsterdom. The other week Fuller, Brennan, Devereaux & the Baxters went down to the station to "see off" Mrs. Fuller & her two daughters on the start of their trip to

England. Returning in Jessops' new station wagon, they
reached Shambazaar, where some guy opened up with a
sub-machine gun from the top of a building. Stopping
the car, they turned around to be met with a hail of rifle
bullets from a party of police, firing past them at the
goondahs, two of whom dropped dead out of the top
windows of the building. Fortunately none of the sahibs
were hit, & the police provided an armoured car escort to
get them onto the Dum Dum Road.

   Another of Jessops' crowd was involved in an incident
during the curfew the other night. Mitchell, our head
Structural draftsman, had been up to Dum Dum to the
Doaks', it was Robbie Doaks' fifth birthday. The Mitchells
left by car at 8:30 pm to return to town. Driving down
Central Avenue they were stopped by a military picket &
the car was searched. Just after they started up again,
some of the soldiers, due to a misunderstanding, opened
up & put six bullets into Mitch's car, bursting two back
tyres, the petrol tank, etc. Mitchell & his wife were
unhurt, but the experience scared the pants off Mitchell
Mem-sahib.

   When Howell heard of the episode, he immediately
renewed his & his family's passports. Poor old Bill, he is
a very timid guy & talks with increasing pessimism of
the state of India. Personally, I think if I were married, I
would leave the country, but being young & single I am
rather interested to see how it will all turn out, & anyway
from what I read of England, I should probably be bored
stiff living there in an ordinary job in the rut.

   You have probably read in the papers that Gandhi is in
Calcutta. Actually he was only passing through, but there
was such a pitched battle raging in the city that he decided
to stay & try to calm things down.

   He & Suhrawardy, the ex-Muslim League Premier of

Homeguard 1940, all men of Ormesby village. Fred is in centre row fourth from left

Fred with Bob Kraus, 1943

Fred at the compound's pool, from letter dated Feb. 3, 1946

Jim Bell 1946

Fred, Jim Bell(?), Bob

The Royal Calcutta Golf Clubhouse, from letter dated June 17, 1947

From letter dated Aug. 12, 1946

No. 10 Post Office Rd., Dum Dum, from letter dated Dec. 6,

L to R: Arthur Dwyer, Parkinson and Jock Farren 1947

The compound pool

Fred's first flat in Dum Dum, 18A Rajabagan

The train to Darjeeling, 1946

From the letter dated June 17, 1947

Viswarkarma Puja in Fred's Dept., 1947

Paul, Jock Farren, Fred & Joan Farren, from the letter dated
Sept. 25, 1947

Children's christmas party, "The Club", Dum Dum, letter dated Dec. 24, 1947

Jessop & Co., Dum Dum

Hindu Temple, Calcutta from letter dated April 19, 1948

Fred, letter dated Jan. 20, 1948

Fred's favourite taxi driver

Fred, Ann & Bob

Fred & Ann on their wedding day

The grave of Fred Turnbull, Fred Brennan and Arthur Dwyer,covered with flowers. St. Paul's Cathdral, Calcutta.

Bengal, decided to stay together in a "bustee"[54] in one of
the worst affected parts of the town, but when angry
crowds demonstrated & pitched bombs at them, they
decided to give up on the idea & moved to Belliaghatta.
Old Gandhi must have been surprised when crowds of
Bengali Hindus swarmed round his bungalow, shouting
to him to "clear off," & the people of both communities of
Noakhali, where he was heading, have told him, "Stay
away, Gandhi, we don't want you in Noakhali." Gandhi
must be an older & wiser man now to see what sort of a
gang he has helped to give "Home Rule" to.

Our four days were spent swimming at the Club, playing billiards & snooker, & catching up on our sleep in the
mornings.

Saturday night, I organized the usual "whist drive" &
dance, but as we were short of one lady to make up the
tables, I played with a lady's card, deducting ten tricks as a
penalty. I was most surprised to find that I had won first
prize even after deducting the ten tricks. A bottle of
whiskey & two bottles of Vermouth prove my card playing must be on the up-grade.

Just lately, the monsoons drawing to a close, we see
snakes almost every day. Our bearer had a narrow escape
when a particularly nasty one got into his godown[55] at
night. Fortunately the croaking of the frog it had caught
in its mouth woke him up, & he killed the snake. The next
day our cook killed another one in the cookhouse, & last
week, as we sat under the palms at the Club having tea, a
crow sitting on the fence was kicking up a hell of a din &
when we went over to see what it was, we spied a big rat
snake, half its body on the grass, the top half twined
round a post & the wire mesh at the top, We called the
durwan[56] but he came running with his "kukri"[57] too late,
the snake vanished in the undergrowth.

Tell Violet I have read three good books during the holidays, which she may find interesting, if she has not already read them: *The Razor's Edge* by Somerset Maugham, *Mother India* by Katherine Mayo (a must, this, to give you some idea of Indian religions), & *Mine own Executioner* by Nigel Baldwin. You see that sometimes I do some book reading, although usually I haven't time & usually I prefer magazines.

The weather is still changeable, with rain & bright intervals, East Bengal & South India have some heavy floods.

So far I haven't decided anything about my holiday. Most of India is too unsettled to contemplate any travelling.

All my friends here are well, including myself; I hope you and the family are the same. Incidentally, it is three and a half years today since I left home. The next one and a half years will soon pass, & I might even be home before that, if the situation turns out bad.

Remember me to the gang.

Aug. 27th

We Britishers in Jessop's have just passed through a difficult period; not a very good beginning for the New India, & incidentally, our Directors handled the situation in a rather tactless manner. Briefly, here is what happened.

Aug. 14th, the day preceding Independence day, the Jessops' directorate issued a circular to the works, stating that as a sort of "Freedom" bonus, workers would receive

a Rs 5/- gift from the firm. No. 1 staff (like myself,
imported from England) got nothing. No. 2 staff (domiciled Europeans, Anglo-Indians, & Indian foremen)
would get Rs 30/-. And No. 3 staff (Departmental head
clerks, regular works' bearers, car drivers & Durwans, that
is Gurkha guards) would receive Rs 10/-.

The workmen, prodded by their Bengali instigated
Union, (which although registered, is not recognized by
the Company) submitted a badly worded petition to the
Directors *demanding* a month's pay as bonus, because
previously they had never had a bonus, even through the
war years when huge profits were made. And unless they
did receive a favourable reply by 10 am on Wed. Aug. 20th
they would take action.

The Company ignored the petition, thinking that as
Jessop's had never had any trouble (thanks to the sahibs
talking to the men) there wouldn't be any serious trouble
on the 20th

After the four days holiday, we resumed work on the
19th Tuesday, & I noticed the men were fairly restless.
However, dead on 10 am on the morning of the 20th
every man stopped his machine, or the work he was
doing, and just sat down on the job.

Incidentally, I was in sympathy with the workers'
demands, although I did not agree with the Bengali
Union, the petition or the sit-down strike. Still I know
that most of the men are half starved, & why shouldn't
they get a decent bonus? They did the work as much
as I did.

Anyway, Sitwell, acting Works' Director (in the
absence of Warren & Irving, now in London) came down
to the works & met the Union (unrecognized) delegates,
where he explained that the Company was in desperate
financial straits, due to riots, strikes in other supplying

firms, & the general unsettled position of the country, finishing his speech by flatly refusing to increase the proposed bonus.

The following day, the men turned up as usual, but remained sitting by their work. Some nasty remarks were passed about the British & the Company's Directors, but most of my men (400 of them) drifted into my office, & rather sheepishly apologized for going on strike, saying they meant no offence to me personally. I surprised them all by agreeing that they should get a month's pay, but gave them hell for taking the law into their own hands. Our three works were at a standstill, the beam & stockyard & Clive St. stores, & following Jessops' lead, Braithwaites' 4000 men & Garden Reach Workshops' 8000 men came out on strike for the same reason. Our stay-in sit-down strike lasted the rest of the week, & up to tiffin time the following Monday, when Sitwell climbed down & offered them a minimum of Rs 10/- per man, & more if other Companies gave more. The men are working as hard as ever, but I feel that the whole thing could have been handled better, although both sides were to blame.

By the way, there are strong rumours that our Chairman of the Board, Warren, & Senior Director Irving are both in England negotiating to sell out the Company, probably to Maswaris.

Due to inclement monsoon weather & the strained atmosphere around Calcutta & Dum Dum, we have spent a very quiet week, although on Thursday during the strike I went into Calcutta with Arthur Dwyer, did some shopping & picked up the Club's month supply of ciga-rettes & booze. We have the radiogram for entertainment, getting good programmes from Ceylon & Australia, & occasionally from London. Every night someone drops

in, John Beard, Kelman, Arthur Dwyer, & we make our
own fun. Last night Bob's Army friend, Ken came in. He
told us that he came up by taxi & the driver, after taking
the fare, asked for some baksheesh, but Ken said, "We're
giving you the ruddy country, what more do you want?"
    While I remember, Mr. Hickie, our Storekeeper,
thanks you very much for the razor blades. He says they
will last him for the rest of his life & he can die clean-
shaven. Actually, he had his horoscope compiled by an
Indian Brahmin, who told him he would die at 72, & he is
68 years old now.
    While I was in town on Thursday, I was struck by the
absence of Europeans from the main streets. Englishmen
are a rarity in this country now, although around Clive St.
(now renamed Netaji Bore St.) there were lines of cars
outside the offices. I called into the National Bank of
India to deposit 5000 chips of Jessops' Club funds. The
Bank is roughly the size of Middlesbrough Town Hall
filled with about 5000 Indians. So I headed for the only
white face I could see, belonging to a Scotsman about my
age. He fixed up my business & I sat & talked to him
about India, etc. for half an hour. I think my Yorkshire
was as pleasant to him as his brogue was refreshing to my
ear.
    Now, translation: Jai Hind means literally, Go India,
or a polite go, forward, onward, Hind, sort of "Forward
India." And Pakistan Zindabad meaning the same as Viva
La France, we have "Live on, Pakistan."
    Since Gandhi came to Calcutta, the rioting has de-
creased, & the two communities now throw rose water at
each other instead of acid. Fred Brennan was in town the
other night & some enthusiastic Indian almost drowned
him with rose water, but Brennan said it didn't smell too
good.

I notice that the Boro started off the season by drop-
ping a point at home, & in the mid-week match, a point at
Sheffield. By the look of the first results the Second
Division teams are playing almost as good football as
First Division, & drawing big crowds too.

Today received a bundle of magazines & a letter from
you with snap enclosed. If Gracie Fields can lounge
around in swimming costumes at fifty, there is still a
chance for you. Also note with interest that New Zealand
is asking for immigrants with free or assisted passages in
some cases.

America & Russia seem determined to start a real argument, while Britain seems to be too concerned with her
economic position to argue. This week should see the
finish of the dollars borrowed from America, a period
when the U.S.A. sank well down in my opinion for driving
such a hard bargain.

Well, next month sees the fine weather come in & the
men's ten day holidays. I don't know whether I shall take
mine yet.

Best wishes to all & Love.

P.S. This seems to be my correct address now:
c/o Jessop & Co.
Dum Dum
24 Parganas
West Bengal, India

Sept. 8th

Still in the land of change & revolution whilst Indian
History, good & bad, is in the making. Last week, after a
riot-free spell, the killing broke out once more as fierce as
ever. Even Gandhi was assaulted by the mob, but police
intervention saved him from serious harm. Incidentally,
his attackers were Bengali Hindus.

Gandhi promptly went on a fast unto death, or until
the goondahs saw the error of their ways & repented.
Either Gandhi's fast, or the fresh reinforcements of troops
& police did the trick & Calcutta is once more fairly calm
& quiet. Gandhi left this morning for the Punjab, where a
full-scale civil war is in progress.

During the trouble last week, a couple of hundred were
killed & many injured. Among the casualties was the old
Muslim "bawarchi" (cook) of the people who live in the
flat below us (the Mitchells). The "bawarchi" lives in
Calcutta & on the night of the riots, left as usual at 5 pm
for his train. Several of my men travel on the same train,
& from one of them, Guffur Mistry, I heard the story.

They all left the train at the station & were passing
through a Hindu area, the old cook first & the others in
ones & twos following. Guffur Mistry related how he saw
a gang of young Hindus at the corner trip up the old
cook, kicking him in the head & stabbing him. The rest of
the Muslims promptly scattered & ran for it (they would
never think of trying to help each other if there is any
danger). Since then, no one has heard anymore about the
old man, so he is probably dead.

Yesterday, Sunday, I had a busy day; during the week

Roberts, the billiard firm man, phoned me to say he & his family would be coming down to Dum Dum for the weekend, weather & riots permitting. Unfortunately, I had been invited to accompany the Farrens to the Scotch Church in Calcutta for the christening of baby Ian, with a christening party to follow in the compound. Anyway, I compromised on Sunday morning by waiting at the Club for the Roberts' & when 11 am came & there was no sign of them, I slipped over to the Farrens' (they had all returned by this time) & drank Ian's health with the crowd: Godfather Alex Smith, the Doaks, the Ewings, the Birchenoughs, E.B. Wilson, the Howell girls, Uncle Tom Cobley & all.[58] At noon I left & went back to the Club to find Mrs. Roberts & her two sons had arrived, accompanied by Mr. Piat & another lady.

Mrs. Roberts is quite young and a good sport, & we were soon swimming in the pool with the two young kids (the first time they had ever been in the water). Mr. Roberts was sick & couldn't come.

There is a story attached to the Mr. Piat; he was manager of Jessops' Structural Works when Howell was only a young assistant. After an argument one day, Howell called Piat a liar, Piat gave him one minute to retract the statement & then bashed him in the mouth, smashing all Howell's front teeth & knocking him cold. Subsequently, Piat got the sack from Jessops, for taking the law into his own hands. He got the manager's job at Robert Hudson's Wagon Works in Calcutta, where he has been ever since.

I had heard stories about the man, but had never met him. He is a magnificent specimen, even now at 68 years of age, a real giant of a man, & I could easily picture him giving Howell a punch in the teeth. Strangely enough, talking to some of the older Indian workmen about him, they said he was a good man, although he thrashed many of them, & they all used to quake in their shoes when he came around. Yet he gave them good wages & got good output. Possibly this is a solution to the India problem.

This next Wednesday we are going into town for dinner at the Roberts', riots & curfews permitting & providing we can fix up transport.

Tuesday 9th
Last night my letter writing was rudely interrupted by the arrival of John Beard, who looks slightly better, but is still suffering from the after-effects of his dysentery.

This week the newspapers printed several new monetary restrictions which have been brought into operation from Sept. 1st. Roughly it means that no individual can take more than 150 chips out of the country, or remit more than that sum to any country in any one month. How this will affect us, no one quite seems to know, so I am waiting for information from my bank, so you will probably not receive the usual allowance this month. I was fortunate in being able to transfer some of my savings home. Also in Violet's recently received letter, she asked me to purchase some books from U.S.A. for her, but there are now several obscure restrictions in operation, to cut down movement of Sterling Area currencies (rupees) to countries outside of the Sterling Area (USA). However, I shall try for the books she requires.

This all seems to be part of Bevins & Daltons' plan to preserve dollars & cut down spending of the British Dominions. Personally, I think it rather severe on a chap like our Fuller, who has just sent his wife & two daughters to Bradford, Yorkshire. Obviously 150 chips per month is not sufficient to support them in England.

Today received a big mail, one from you, one from

Ernie Cooper, one from Jack Simpson saying that he has got a job as foreman plater with his old firm, Wright Anderson in Gateshead. £8 per week, with a substantial raise after six months if he is suitable. Jack says that he is as badly off in Gateshead as he was in Dum Dum. He is living in "digs," & his wife is still in Rotherham, & the housing shortage is so acute that he is likely to remain like that for years, he says.

I have got the address of the Labour & Employment bureaux in Wellington N.Z. from Jock Farren & as Bob Kraus has since become keen, we intend writing for prospects in the near future.

After a week of fine weather the "rains came" again & flooded recently dried up roads & fields once more. I suppose the news of the week in Dum Dum is the fact that Birch, Jock Farren, Arthur Dwyer, Bill Howell & myself have all gone teetotal. I was very amused to see all the memsahibs worried about it. As much as they disliked & played hell about the boys drinking, now they have stopped the "mems" are very unhappy about it, & have even gone so far as to buy & bring whiskey into the houses to try & bring the boys back to normal.

Joan Farren leaves for England at the beginning of October. Mrs. Smith & daughter Maureen are expected out then, & Alex Smith is once more coming to live out at Dum Dum.

My best wishes to you-all, hope all my letters reach you (there is a Postal strike in Bombay). The recent news of England makes me more inclined to stay abroad.

Sept. 18th

After at least six attempts, I am really getting down to
letter writing; during the last ten days we have had a lot of
fun, & I have thoroughly enjoyed myself.

Last weekend, Walter Brooks, one of our Structural
foremen, invited us over to his place in Calcutta for the
weekend, with a dance on the Saturday night. Bob & I
had already arranged to visit the Roberts' in town (the
billiard man) where we were to have dinner.

Borrowing the Works' car, we set off in the afternoon,
taking our dress suits in a suitcase, & arrived at the
Roberts' at 6 pm.

Very soon Bob & Roberts were engrossed in a game of
billiards, while I sat & talked to Mrs. Roberts, explaining
that we would have to leave early so as to meet the gang in
the dance. Mrs. Roberts is a good sport, one of girls, &
she persuaded me to play the piano, & we sang some
Webster Ziegler & Ann Booth[59] together. The piano playing was murderous, including some one finger stuff in
parts.

Within an hour all sorts of peculiar types had drifted in,
including a girl named Rose (a local beauty specialist or
something), but she was a first-rate pianist. There was an
Anglo-Indian with a smashing baritone voice, Mrs.
Roberts sang soprano, my tenor (?), Bob's falsetto
(falsetto teeth), Mr. Roberts' base & Rose's contralto.
Quite honestly there was some wizard singing, all the old
music hall ballads like "Rose of Tralee," & most of the
Gilbert & Sullivan pieces, like the Gondoliers. I was quite
sorry when we broke up for dinner, & all the types were

most enthusiastic, saying that they had only intended
staying for five minutes & that they hadn't enjoyed a
sing-song like that for years.

Consequently, we have a standing invitation to dine at
half a dozen homes in Calcutta.

After dinner we changed into our tuxedos, said goodbye to the Roberts', caught a taxi at 11 pm & set off for our
blind date at the Ordnance Club dance. As we swept
through the Calcutta maidan, six miles of cool open grass
& park to Hastings, where the dance was held, we both
wondered what sort of girls Walter Brooks had fixed up
for us as partners. Actually, we needn't have worried.
They were three wizard dancers, good fun, intelligent &
easy on the eyes too.

From 1:30 pm until 3 am I didn't miss one dance, & got
a real kick out of the whole evening. The food, drinks &
floor show was excellent & made up for all the dances we
have missed (this was the first real dance we had attended
since New Year's Day).

We stayed the night with Walter, sleeping on a mattress
on the floor, very comfortable. Next morning, the dog
awoke me, licking my face. We breakfasted & when
Walter's pal came round in his car, we set off for Dum
Dum, picking up two of the girls on the way. We spent the
day in wonderful weather, swimming, having tiffin & tea
under the palms in the open.

Later in the evening after dark we all walked round to
see Walter's mother & father. A retired engineer, his father
is leaving the country to live in Australia, & probably
going on to New Zealand if he can find a house. With the
house behind us we all sat on the lawn in deck chairs, &
watched the moon climb over the jungle, with the scent
of flowering shrubs in the air, the howls of jackals, & the
shrill whine of the myriads of insects. India at its best, we

sat & drank our coffee & talked of the world & India, servants, housing, what we all wanted from life, while the mosquitoes got what they wanted from biting my legs.

Returning to the Clubhouse, we swam in the moon- light & finished off with dancing to the gramophone on the verandah.

Monday night, I had decided to write this letter & had just started when Beard arrived in his car & barged into my room, shouting, "Come on, you lousy pair of stay-at-homes, we are going out to dinner." So I had to get a quick shave & change to preserve the peace & we drove the nineteen miles to Barrackpore, where we called in to the Royal Hotel, a sort of roadhouse. Everything else pales into insignificance when I remember the beef- steak, rarely done, soaked in gravy, tender, succulent, melting in the mouth, the most delicious steak I have ever consumed in this country. In fact, I would walk that nine- teen miles for such a meal.

We came back to Dum Dum at 2 am. The drive from Barrackpore on the smooth straight road between the jungle verge is wonderful.

Tuesday night we spent in our darkroom developing & printing the snaps we took on Sunday, & there are some remarkably good ones, too.

Wednesday was Viswarkarma Puja, the "Tool Puja," when the workmen bring their gods into the works, deco- rate the machines & cranes with streamers & leaves & have music & singing all day. My Department was the only place to have a real Tamasha, so I invited Jock & Joan Farren, Birch & his wife, & Arthur Dwyer, to the cere- mony. Plenty of beer & whiskey provided, a magician's show, & we got some really good snaps of the Brahmin priests blessing the machines etc. Joan Farren enjoyed the show immensely, & was tickled to death when some of my mistries got drunk. One of them, Dhiren, an opium addict & one of my top men, although very small has a face like old Bill of the first Great War. During the magician's show, the conjuror referred to me as "the boss" (I was singled out for special attention, being the head of the Department), so when Dhiren had had a few drinks (enough to kill a horse), he staggered round wearing a Gandhi cap saying, "He iss my boss," and finishing up by bursting into tears. This is the first English I have ever heard him speak. Joan couldn't forget it, & she was still giggling over it when I saw her last night in the Club.

We are going round to the Farrens' for dinner on Monday night, a sort of farewell, as Joan sails for England the 6th of Oct.

In your letter you made two horrible mistakes. The foundry foremen's job, salary Rs 300 per month, £97-10s; as 300 chips = 100 x 1 s-6d, or 450 shillings, or £22-10s, I think the 300 chips should be Rs 1300. Also Calcutta is *West* Bengal, not East. East Bengal is Pakistan, & as I live in Hindusthan, the alteration to my address is the addition of West before Bengal.

Thanks for the Poly-fotos, brother! You aren't fat, you're colossal. I wouldn't like to be a beetle in Avonholme.[60] Note that your heat wave still persists, 75 degrees, phwew, & I am shivering in 90 degrees in the shade.

You can probably get some idea of what is happening in the Punjab when you read that one million refugees have been evacuated; fortunately Calcutta still remains quiet.

Best wishes to all at home.

Sept. 25th

Behind with my letter writing again because of the few
evenings I stay in the bungalow. However, as a peace
offering I enclose some of our latest snaps, developed &
printed by Bob. Taken at the Viswarkarma Puja in my
Department, they enable you to become one of the privi-
leged few who have witnessed some of the rites of the
Hindu religion.

No. 1 shows the Brahmin priest blessing piles of fruit,
etc. ready for the feast, in front of Viswarkarma, the lady
with four arms sitting on the elephant. (I think she usually
has six arms, but probably she is rationed these days).

The second snap shows us at the magician's show at the
same Puja. Left to right are: Paul (B.Sc. Edinborough),
Jock Farren, myself & Joan Farren, with a sprinkling at
the back of the workmen & their children. I don't know
why I was looking so sorry for myself, possibly the
thought of having to eat the local Indian sweetmeats
made from sour buffalo's milk after the performance.

In your last letter I received your photographs of
Violet. She looks as thin as you look fat; what's the trouble, are you eating her rations?

I have asked Bill Howell for my usual yearly leave,
which he granted, throwing in a few extra days for luck,
from Oct. 11th up to Nov. 3rd, 23 days. I am off to the
seaside again, if I can get accommodation at Golpalpur,
which seems to be about the only part of India not having
any riots.

All the local crowd are working or staying at home next
month, so *unfortunately* I will have to put up with the

company of a lady friend of mine. Actually she is a really
nice girl, a Bachelor of Science too, Mathematics, Physics
& Chemistry, but that doesn't make her any less of a good
sport.

Now, about my allotment home: by sending off several
letters to my bank, & by filling in hundreds of forms for
the Reserve Bank of India, I have managed to carry on
sending the money. But remember, from now on you are
a widow with a wooden leg or something, because I had
to state the reason for the remittance.

Sorry about Violet's books, but I'm afraid that I can't
manage them, dollars being a foreign currency & outside
of Empire regulations.

Since commencing this letter, l have had a reply from
Gopalpur, stating that rooms have been booked for me,
so I am all set for a real three weeks vacation, far away
from work.

Last weekend, persuaded by the Bachelor of Science,
Ann, I swapped my usual dress of shorts & shirt for a stiff
shirt & dinner jacket, & went dancing in Calcutta.
Booking the works' car to take me in Saturday afternoon,
on the way I picked up Westmoreland, the Aluminium
Company manager. "Westy" had hit a bamboo structure
on Independence Day with his car &, as it was out of
commission, had phoned me for a lift into town.

"Westy" is talking of packing in & going to East Africa,
as manager of a firm there. I don't see much of his crowd
these days, his wife is staying in Naini Tal, & Bob
Embleton B.E.M. is living a quiet life. His wife Kathleen
has just flown home to allow Embleton Junior to be born
in England. Bill & Jean Muir, the other young couple
from the Air Survey, have just returned from Alleppo
(Syria) & although I haven't seen them yet, I expect to
meet them at the Club this week.

To get back to my Saturday outing, as I had some time
to spare, I accompanied "Westy" round to the Outram
Club where we played billiards until 6 pm, when I left.
Catching a taxi, I collected Ann outside of the Metro
Cinema, & carried on to her house. She had to iron my
dress suit, because I came down in whites with the tuxedo
bundled up in brown paper.

The night club we visited, "Prince's," had an excellent
orchestra, floor show & food, & although the heat was
intense, I thoroughly enjoyed it. I only missed one dance,
when I was busy with a large beefsteak. Even after being
tied up in Dum Dum for so many months, I found that I
knew lots of the girls & many of the men there. Two of
the girls in the cabaret remembered me, too, & came over
to talk, so Ann just wouldn't believe me when I said I
didn't get around much.

We left at 1 am &, after seeing her home, I debated
whether it was worthwhile paying ten rupees for a taxi to
Dum Dum & again on the Sunday morning, because I
had to come in to town again, as we had arranged to go
swimming. Finally I drifted into Calcutta's Grand Hotel
& got a room for the night for Rs 21. After giving instructions to the bearer to call me at ten in the morning, I slept
like a top, without a mosquito net. Next morning I was so
hungry I almost ate the bearer too when he brought in my
breakfast.

Checking out at 11 o'clock, I called for Ann once more
& we spent the day swimming with the gang at Dum
Dum; a really wizard weekend.

The monsoons are almost over, & the sun shines most
days now very hot & strong during the day, but the nights
are wonderful & cool, just the weather for moonlight
swimming parties. Since Independence Day, Bengal has
come under Indian Standard time; stupid actually,

because even under Bengal time, darkness came at 6:30 pm; but now it is dark at 5:30 pm & we lose the two hours of cool daylight which is the best part of the Indian day.

Oct. 4th is Mahatma Gandhi's birthday, & an official holiday for Hindustan. We have arranged to go by ferry to the Botanical Gardens for a picnic.

The Punjab is still in a troubled state & things seem to be very serious, especially as our local papers seem to be suppressing the news of riots, etc. Calcutta remains quiet & the general atmosphere is much better these days. With the Indians I have come into contact with, politeness & courtesy are shown to everyone, & especially to the sahibs.

There is a good chance for this country if only the leaders would climb down a bit, or take a more sensible view. There is still a lot of communal hatred stirred up in speeches.

Howell has been sick for the past three days & has been absent from work. Also Duke, the manager of the Wagon Works, is in hospital, so Bob & I have the Works (Structural) to ourselves once more. The output is getting better, although I suspect we will have some more trouble over the shortage of rice rations soon.

Best wishes to you all

Gopalpur
Oct. 13th

Sorry to be so behind with my letter writing, but I have had so much to do this last week I didn't even manage a night in the bungalow. However, I have finally arrived at the seaside (or ocean-side), & find that all the Indians, fishermen, bearers, shopkeepers, etc. still remember me. In fact they were all very pleased to see me, most of the regular British sahibs having left the country. Yalton Hall & all the local hotels & boarding houses are now Indian owned.

We, that is Ann & I, arrived yesterday, after the four hundred mile train journey from Howrah Station, then eleven miles from Berhampur by station wagon, passing the blue hills (Eastern Ghats), the green paddy fields & the red roads of South India.

I really needed this holiday, away from the sticky atmosphere of Bengal. Here the air is fresh & clean, the local people are friendly & honest, & still prefer the sahibs to stay rather than to be governed by Indians. We are staying at the Peace Haven Hotel, which is rather old, but clean. It is right on the top of the sand dunes facing the sea, & through the night I can hear the boom & crash of the waves & breakers on the beach.

The weather is rather unsettled, with the tail end of the monsoons sending dark clouds & heavy showers. However, within a couple of days it should clear up.

Yesterday we walked along the beach for miles, then branched off over the sandhills into the casuarina groves, among the custard apple bushes & prickly pear cactus. I wish you could see some of the scenery round Gopalpur. It is much more majestic than the English coast. The sea is louder and more awe-inspiring, the mountains & clouds magnificent, & the catamarans & fishermen picturesque & jungli looking. The place is much quieter than when I was here before, although all the hotels are full. The occupants are mostly Indians & wealthy Bengalis who don't swim or go out to sea in catamarans. They don't run dances or have as much fun as the Europeans do, being much more careful with their money.

Everything is cheap & plentiful here. Food, unrationed cloth, leather sandals, lace work, & in the small shops in the bazaar, goods which went off the Calcutta market months ago are in plentiful supply. Even camera film can be obtained, & yesterday whilst scrounging around the cloth shops, Ann bought some American dress material which is unobtainable anywhere else in India.

This morning I was up at 6:30 am, & after chota-hazri (small breakfast), was in the sea at 7 am. The waves were very rough & I got knocked about a bit, but it was good fun & I stayed in the water for an hour. As usual, we had two fishermen with us to give us the dope on currents, when to dive under a wave or when to jump & float along with it. The waves here are like the side of a house, hundreds of tons of water coming in like an express train. You can imagine what would happen if they hit you unawares. Actually, swimming here can be very danger-ous unless one knows the ropes.

Already I am black again with the sun & wind, & after three weeks of this life, lounging around in swimming trunks or shorts, I should be a nice ebony hue. Three whole weeks away from Jessop & Co. will give me time to forget completely all about work & the Dum Dum life.

Just continue writing to Dum Dum. Letters may go astray if sent here. Then on my return I can spend a day going through all my mail.

The hotel is rather like an old English farm house, high ceilings with rafters & teak beams, scrubbed stone floors & tiled roof. Part of the building was destroyed by a cyclone many years ago. The food is good & plentiful, & naturally we get a lot of fresh fish, crabs, shrimps, lobsters, shellfish, done in a variety of ways.

I miss the old air letter forms. They were just the thing,

I could sit down & knock one off in ten minutes.
However, I shall try to find time for letter writing.
  Best wishes to all the family.

Oct. 27th

Almost the end of my leave, we are returning on the 31st
& the weather is now absolutely perfect; I will be really
sorry to go. The three weeks has done me a lot of good, &
I have put on weight after the good food & fresh air we
get here.

  This morning my fishermen awoke me at 6:30 am &
after putting on my swim trunks, I called Ann & with the
fishermen we walked four miles along the beach to the
next village where they had put out a six mile net. This is
the time of year when the local Indians use this method of
catching fish. The net, attached at both ends to long
ropes, is dropped out to sea by men in surf boats & catamarans, lying in a huge semi-circle. Wooden floats on the
top & lead weights on the bottom keep the net vertical, &
then all the villagers grab hold of the ropes &, marching
up the sands to the sand dunes, drag the net the two miles
back to shore, encircling any fish in that area. As the last
lengths of net near the shore, the water within its half
circle boils & swirls as the fish try to escape. The Indians
shout & chant, anoint their heads with seawater & call on
their gods to provide a big catch.

  It is quite exciting as the last of the long loop of net
comes ashore. Big fish jump out, the Indians rush into the
breakers to prevent them, & the whole makes a wonderful
sight. This morning we watched three nets dragged out;
the catch included: hilsa, beckti, mango fish, pomfret,

stingrays, flatfish, crabs, jellyfish, eels, in fact, different colours & kinds too numerous to mention. Actually today was the first of the big net operations this year, & not many fish were caught.

I have been swimming in the sea practically every day. It is something I never tire of doing. The life here really appeals to me, it is so open & healthy, & the Telagu Indians are such friendly people that it is a pleasure to be in their company.

I mentioned that the sea had been very rough, in a previous letter. My fishermen said it was due to a cyclone somewhere in the Bay of Bengal. They were correct, too, because from letters I have received from Calcutta, they have had cyclonic storms over the city, so it must have crossed the coast further north.

The snaps I am enclosing are: No. 1, one of Ann sitting on the wall of our hotel overlooking the beach, with the coastguard station & a few cottages of Gopalpur behind her.

No. 2 is a snap of our fishermen, Jacky & Jimmy, with the chokra who looks after our towels, etc. when we swim. The boys, Jacky & Jimmy are wearing the pointed straw hats that they use to break the face of the waves. They are terrifically strong, wiry men & can swim for hours without tiring. They know all the currents & whirlpools, when to dive, when to jump. In fact, they are absolutely worthy of having peoples' lives placed in their hands.

No. 3 is a snap of me taking it easy on the beach. Behind me is a sand dune & the building is part of the Palm Beach Hotel. The sun is so bright that it is impossible to see without glare glasses at mid-day, & I couldn't lay long in this position, as the sand is red hot. We have a bamboo hut on the sand to sit in as a shelter against the sun.

No. 4 is a snap of Ann & myself with part of the Peace
Haven buildings, where we are staying, behind us. They
don't look very grand, but they are built more to with-
stand cyclones than for exterior beauty. Acutally, there
are four cottages joined together to form a long row of
rooms, with the dining hall & lounge at one end, slightly
larger & higher than the rest.

Snap no. 5 is of me with my fishermen, taken at 4:30
pm when the tide is out and the water is almost calm.
Unfortunately I can't take any close-ups of the big breakers that come in during the day, because I would have to
stand at the bottom of the sloping beach to take them, &
the wave would bowl me & the camera over.

Anyway, I am leaving it all on Friday, making the third
of three marvelous holidays spent in India, each one quite
worth waiting a year for.

Tonight we are going up to the Palm Beach Hotel for
dancing again. Mr. & Mrs. Fred Baines from Cossipore
Club are staying there, although they complain of the
cost, 32 rupees a day, & drinks, etc. on top of that. Where
I am staying it is only 9 rupees a day or 17 rupees double.

I am looking forward to getting back to Dum Dum to
open all my mail. I haven't had any sent on to me here.
Best wishes to all the family.

Nov. 10

The first opportunity I have had for letter writing since
I came back from leave. My time has been completely
filled in with work & play, & much has happened in Dum

Dum since I left for Gopalpur. Just as an indication of the trend which is developing in Indian industry, I quote the following instance. It happened during the Saturday morning, a week after I had left. A gang of rough looking Hindustanis entered Bob's office & politely told him not to leave the Works or to attempt to leave. At the same time another gang assembled on the verandah & sat down in a half circle round each of Howell's office doors. Howell told them to "clear off" back to their work. They replied saying that they would keep him in his office until the firm sanctioned a month's pay as bonus to every daily paid workman.

Howell again asked to be allowed to pass, which the men refused. Then Howell tried to force his way through them. One of the men claimed that Howell had kicked him & a tremendous shout went up: "Marro, Marro, Marro, Sala!" or, in English, "Hammer the so & so!"

Howell was badly scared & retired into his office while the rest of the workmen downed tools & collected at the office, shouting for Howell's blood. Howell phoned the Dum Dum police, & a Bengali Inspector & twenty men arrived by lorry. Howell demanded protection & asked them to make him a path through the crowd. The Inspector said that, as employees of Jessops, the men had every right to be there & they hadn't actually assaulted him, so he refused to take any action, & withdrew the police from the Works.

The men still shouted insults & threats at Howell, so he phoned the Directors, who immediately granted a month's bonus to the workmen, & the uproar subsided, as the workers went back to their jobs shouting "Jai Hind!"

This "Satyagraha"[61] as the Indians call it, has been used at Shalimar Co., Turner Morrisons, Balmer Lauries,

Burma Shell, & several other firms. Jessops' Directors
were held in their offices by the Clive Street Indian staff
until they granted a bonus. At Balmer Lauries the Works'
Manager was beaten up by the mob when his Directors
refused the bonus; & at a firm at Barrackpore, the
manager escaped from his office, was chased through the
Works by the men, over the boundary wall & into the
jungle. The Bengal Assembly has put Satyagraha on the
agenda for *discussion* at the next meeting of the House.

As I am writing now, there is a Communist meeting in
the Bazaar, using cars with loud speakers. A couple of
Bengalis, Thakur & Chatterjhee, after just being released
from ten years in jail, are stirring up the crowd with their
propaganda. They are shouting into the microphone in
Hindi & Bengali the same old Bolshevik stuff: "Why
should three or four Englishmen own a big workshop like
this, while you haven't enough rice to fill your stomach?"
You can imagine, Mam, what an effect this sort of talk has
on the minds of jungli uneducated cookes, when in
England, even educated people believe it.

I am afraid that India has "had it." Things are getting
worse, & with a war in Kashmir, a war in the Punjab, &
distrust everywhere else in India, strikes, riots, bribery,
swindling & stirring up trouble in every walk of life, India
will collapse. In Dum Dum, at an old R.A.F. training
camp, now used as a headquarters of the National Guard,
hundreds of young men attend every night for drilling,
rifle & bayonet practise, & with their black hats, white
shirts & khaki shorts, remind me of the Nazi youth. The
Indian leaders are very silent lately. The situation seems to
be out of their control, while food & cloth supplies for
the average Indian are becoming increasingly more
difficult to obtain.

However, enough of trouble. My life remains interest-

ing & all my men were very pleased to see me back & are
extremely polite to me.

I have just had to do something very distasteful, that is,
stop sending money home to you. After my holiday,
buying a new winter suit & other clothes, annual bill to
the Swimming Club, etc. my bank balance has lately
rapidly diminished. However, you can always use my
money from the bank at home if you need it.

Mrs. Smith & Maureen (wife & daughter of Alex) are
in Bombay & expect to reach Calcutta tomorrow. They
are going to stay with the Birchenoughs. Mrs. Farren is in
England now, of course, & Mr. & Mrs. Ewing have just
returned from leave in Darjeeling where they have been
stranded because of a Railway & taxi strike for two weeks.

The other night I was talking to Mrs. Howell at the
Club, & she told me that they were going home as quickly
as possible. She had contacted Alf Perry about accomoda-
tion on Tees-side. She didn't say if Bill was going, or if
they intended to return to India. She was surprised too,
when I told her that Ernie Perry had left for South Africa.
She said she hadn't heard from him in three years, except
for one enquiry about the job in Jessops.

Bob & I have been getting into town quite a lot lately
for dances & the cinema; & this weekend I went in to
meet Ann on Saturday afternoon. We went round for tea
to the house of the girl we met in Gopalpur, Evelyn. She
lives in a flat with her two sisters. I quite enjoyed it. There
was I listening to four girls discussing coats, costumes,
dresses, materials, patterns, etc. etc. & I couldn't get a
word in sideways.

After tea, Ann & I had dinner at a Chinese joint, then
finished up at the Ordnance Club dance out at Hastings.
Bob & I stayed at Spencer's Hotel that night & next
morning, Sunday, Ann came round, dragged me out of

bed & made me go to St. Andrew's Scottish Church with
her (my first visit for years). Then we went round to an
address we picked up in the newspaper where there was a
piano for sale. Ann plays very well, & after trying it out,
she bought it for 450 chips (very cheap for India).
Catching a taxi we arrived at Dum Dum for tiffin &
stayed the day at the Club.

   I am pleased to hear that you have received the lace
dishcloths (or whatever they are), but have no other mail
from you mentioning photographs taken on leave.
Altogether I sent ten letters with snaps enclosed to
Avonholme. I sincerely hope that our mail isn't being
lost. My best wishes to all the gang, & all the family. I see
you are all going anti-Labour at the Municipal Elections.

Nov. 25th

At present I have lots to write about, but no time to write.
Once more after several days I am having a quiet night in
the bungalow & getting some news down on paper for
the benefit of my friends at home.

   Local Dum Dum news in brief is that: Jock Farren has
just come out of hospital where he has been for a week
after an attack of *measles*. Bill Howell has had three days
off work; he seems very depressed these days & suffers
from gout & stomach trouble. I think I mentioned that
Mrs. Smith & young Maureen have arrived & are living
with Alex at the other daughter's place in the compound
(the Birchenoughs).

   Our managing director, P.F.S. (Patsy) Warren, has

returned from a nine months' stay in England. He & his
wife were up at the Howells' yesterday for tiffin. Patsy was
over at the Club & played snooker with the boys.

I have had an enjoyable weekend & have been around a
lot. After leaving work on Saturday (incidentally, Sat. was
the Hindu Puja of Jagadhattri, but we worked), I packed
up my suit & a change of clothes in a small suitcase & set
off for Calcutta. The journey took some time because of
all the processions carrying the Hindu gods around the
streets, but eventually I arrived at Ann's flat. We had tea
together in town & visited some friends, where I picked
up a couple of guest tickets for the Ordnance Club Dance.
The Ordnance Club has had orders to close down because
all the British troops & Ordnance workers have left India;
so the Club had a farewell dance with everything free, but
only members & guests allowed.

We thoroughly enjoyed the dance & cabaret, although
the floor was packed, even when we left at 2:30 am.
Coming back from Hastings by taxi alongside of the river
& wharves, the night (or rather, early morning) was very
cold.

I stayed the night at Ann's place, her mother having
fixed me up with a bed in the dining room. They awoke
me at 7 am because we had arranged to go on a picnic. At
7 am I didn't want any picnic, I wanted another 48 hours
in bed, but Ann & her mother dragged me out. At 8:30
Doreen, one of Ann's office friends, arrived & the three of
us set off looking for a taxi, while I looked like a pack
mule, loaded up with coats, baskets & thermos flasks. We
caught a taxi to a little place named Mahjerat, about three
miles out of the city. It is the terminus of a local light railway. The Bengali station master put on a special first class
carriage for us (no one ever travels first class on this railway) & the toy engine was coupled up & we set off on the

28 mile journey to Falta, through the Sunderbans & tiger
country, down the river towards Diamond Harbour. This
railway is similar to the Darjeeling-Himalayan metre
gauge railway, & the journey lasted three hours.

We were the only Europeans to travel that way for
some time evidently, & all the Indians were very friendly
& helpful. Our carriage was quite comfortable, electricity
& fans, & only the three of us & Ann's spaniel as the occupants.

Falta is a rather lonely, but pretty spot on the banks of
the Hooghly near the mouth of the river. There is an
ancient ruined fort there, first used by the British in the
days of Raja Serazud-dowlah, the Indian ruler of Bengal.
The fort is built on an island on the banks of the river, & is
encircled by a huge moat one hundred yards wide. Old
cannon emplacements & watch towers are all that is left of
it, with a well & a row of tumbled-down barrack huts.

We entered the fort over the ancient draw-bridge,
complete with original chains, weights & spikes. Inside is
the Dak-bungalow, a fairly modern building, also being
used as an inspection centre for the area shipping authorities. We didn't use the Dak-bungalow, but had lunch
under a banyan tree. I put some hard work in with a tin
opener.

After lunch we scrounged around taking photographs
& watching a couple of Indians tapping coconut trees to
draw off the syrup which, after fermenting, is made into
"toddy," the local fierce alcoholic drink. The water in the
moat looked very clear & inviting, being fresh (it has an
outlet into the Hooghly river). The afternoon sun was
warm, too, so when the girls withdrew, I undressed &
went into the water in my underpants. The water was
grand & the spaniel came in with me. As the moat was
very deep, I had to keep swimming while I held onto my

underpants, which were coming off. When the time came to get out, the too-wicked women refused to go, & as my underpants were aertex type, I wasn't keen on getting out while the so & so's stood & laughed. Eventually Ann threw me some large leaves, which I coyly arranged, & I sidled out, but the two female tormentors were both taking my photograph as hard as they could go.

It was quite an enjoyable day. We came back by the same train at 4 pm, arriving in Calcutta after dark at 7 o'clock. We got a taxi back to Ann's flat, where Bob was waiting for me. Ann collected some clothes, & we three set off for Dum Dum. After dinner at our bungalow, Ann & I went round to Freddy Brennan's house to a party. The Doaks, Birchenoughs, Smiths, Jock Farren, Fuller, Walter Brooks, Baxters, & a few unknowns were there (also Arthur Dwyer). We danced to piano, guitar & saxophone. Mrs. Smith was hopping round like a two year old; she told me she was glad to be back in India. England & Scotland were too stiff & starchy for her & Maureen.

Ann & I left at 1:30 am & came back to our bungalow. I slept the night in the spare bedroom (Jack Simpson's old room), & was bitten to hell with mosquitoes. We only had two nets, one used by Bob & the other on my bed, where Ann slept.

Next morning at 7:30 am (I was dog tired with all the late nights), Alex Smith called round in his car to take us into town. Monday was a holiday, the Muslim feast of Mohorrum, but Alex was working & Ann had to go to the office in the morning. After breakfast I took her round to the office & then scrounged around Calcutta watching the processions of Muslims carrying their "Tazias"[62] down to the river.

During the afternoon we went to the New Empire to see the film "Nora Prentiss," quite a good show. Anyway, lately I have had a lot of fun, & getting around once more makes a pleasant change after all the time we were cut off from Calcutta because of riots, etc. Give my best wishes to the family. Keep fit.

Dec. 2nd

Only three more weeks to Xmas with plenty of work & play in the future for me. The work part is due to an easing of the ban on Indian Rail transport. As a consequence of this, we are getting supplies of raw steel & materials, & are able to dispatch what we fabricate too. There is less tension among Jessops' labour also, & the men are working more whole-heartedly, which all means more work for me, as we are very short-handed with regard to supervisory staff.

The last week I have been busier than at any time in my previous three and three-quarter years in India. The amount of jobs, orders in the shops, is colossal. We seem to be rebuilding the whole of India: bridges, factories, Hydro-electric power plant & spillways, chemical tanks & steelworks plant, cranes, gantries, wagons, road-rollers, passenger coaches, chimneys, vats, pit-head gear, mine arches, textile & sugar mills, blast furnaces, stagings, piles, jetties, & also we are extending our own shops & plant.

Most of my time is spent with inspectors. This morning, for instance, at 8 o'clock, Merz & McLellan inspector Moss arrived to pass boiler flooring for Cossipore Electric Supply project. Then the I.S.D. inspector, Roy, wanted

me with him while he passed four completed hopper
wagons. Then another inspector arrived for passing
a huge gas tank for Sindri Power Gas Co. (all these
drawings made by Ashmore Benson & Pease at Stockton-
on-Tees). Then another I.S.D. inspector came in to pass
two strengthened crane girders for a Government factory
at Ishapore. Still, it is good to realize that we are once
more getting some production & output.

The weather is perfect, clear cold nights with a
wonderful full moon; warm at mid-day. The most healthy
weather of the Indian seasons, apart from frequent colds,
due to the sudden changes in temperature in the
evenings.

I haven't heard from you in some time, but everyone
seems to be in the same boat, awaiting letters from home.
There seems to be some stoppage in the mails. Life is
brightening up for we Europeans in India, although
petrol rationing is very strict & restrictions on alcohol are
coming into force soon, while the rise in prices of every
commodity continues.

However, we get a lot of fun, & I am often in Calcutta.
Last Saturday Ann & I were having dinner in Firpo's, & I
met about 100 people that I knew, among them, Jimmy
Bell & his wife. Jimmy is working as an engineer in a
cotton mill at Budge Budge; he has invited us over for
New Year. I also met Rabbitts, the horrible type from our
Clive Street office, who sat next to me at Jessops' Golf
Luncheon. Bert Whiteside was there too, who left Jessops
to work for Brooke Bonds Tea Company.

Just across the dance floor from me was young Chota
Ford, now wearing a bushy ginger beard. He used to be
the special pilot of ex-premier Suhrawardy's private plane,
& has just come back from where he has been on a job.

Last Sunday I had another eventful day. Bob & I had

been into town on Saturday, & we stayed the night at the
Great Eastern Hotel. Rising early, I picked up Ann & we
set off for Dum Dum. The sun was hot enough for a swim
& we stayed in the water until noon. Bill Howell has
improved in health during the last few days & he was
beating it up in the Club with the boys. All the Jessops
crowd was there, & we had a good session of snooker.
Ann joined Mrs. Howell & the other mem-sahibs with
their knitting under the palms on the lawn. At tiffin in our
bungalow, we had the usual crowd of young folks along
for the meal. It is good fun to have our own house with a
crowd of people talking, laughing, playing the
radio-gram, or down on the court playing badminton.

Ann & I left for Calcutta early in the afternoon, as we
had a party to go to in town. You will probably remember
me mentioning in a previous letter Evelyn Feegrade, the
girl who lived in the same Hotel at Gopalpur, her sister
Yvonne, & Jean (Jan) the French officer who accompanied us to the Barbecue at the Palm Beach Hotel. The
party was for Yvonne's 21st birthday, held at Jean's flat.
Strangely enough, there was a guy there whom I knew,
named Sloss, a Dundee Scot & a friend of Jimmy Bell's.
There was any amount of whiskey, white wine (whine) &
champagne. I came home at midnight in a jeep with
Evelyn, Sloss & Ann to keep me company. After a visit to
Jessops' Club to show Sloss & Evelyn the swimming pool
& tennis courts, they dropped me & returned to Calcutta.

Incidentally, during the party, while I was talking to
Jean (I don't know how I managed it, for he can hardly
speak any English), he told me his father & mother came
from Metz, he was born in Luxembourg, his sister in
Holland, a brother in Germany, a brother in Belgium, &
the youngest girl in France. His father was a travelling
engineer, erecting bridges.

During visits to the cinema lately, I have seen "Humouresque," "Sinbad the Sailor," & "The Razor's Edge." The last named was not up to the standard of the book in my opinion.

Last night was our Lodge of Instruction meeting, tonight the Club entertainments committee meeting. Wednesday is my night for writing letters, & Thursday I am off to Calcutta to the Y.W.C.A. dance, so all my time is filled in. On me has fallen the job of organizing the children's party at the Club on Dec. 21st, sports, etc. On Dec. 14th we are having a get-together & tennis party & a dance on the 21st.

This afternoon at work a youngish, fat Englishman called to see me. A cockney named Tommy Baker, he has been in this country four months, & is the factory manager of a new Company starting up at Dum Dum, manufacturing stainless steel & copper tanks. He was looking for accommodation in Dum Dum & heard that we had a spare room (Jack Simpson's old room). However, we couldn't do anything for him, as Jessops wouldn't consider taking an outsider into one of their bungalows. Actually, it would have been okay with us if it could have been arranged, as he has a car & a motor bike & could solve our transport problem. He painted a very black picture of England with restrictions & shortages, & said he was glad to get away from it. I hope you don't find things too bad, & can find time for some fun. My best wishes to the family & Love.

[enclosed clipping from newspaper:]

POLICE DISPERSE CROWD FROM CALCUTTA CINEMA
by a Staff Reporter
    The police had to use tear gas and make lathi charges

yesterday morning to disperse a crowd of over 3,000
persons from the precincts of the Lighthouse Cinema,
Calcutta, where the film version of a well-known Bengali
novel is showing.

From early morning a large crowd gathered outside
the cinema to buy tickets, all of which had previously
been sold out. Despite a "House Full" sign, the crowd
invaded the premises when the cinema opened and clam-
oured for admission. Ticket holders were stopped and not
allowed to enter the hall.

Rai Sahib S. Brahmachari, Deputy Commissioner of
Police, Central District, repeatedly appealed to the crowd
to leave the cinema peacefully, but without success. A
police party then dispersed the crowd with mild lathi
charges and two tear gas bombs.

People in the crowd threw brickbats at the building,
and damaged some of its plate glass doors.

Dec. 8th

Monday evening, & a chance for me to write a few letters
& to recuperate after another energetic weekend. As usual
on Saturday afternoon I went into town to meet Ann. She
had refused to tell me where we were going, so at 6 pm
when we set off, I hadn't the slightest idea where we were
heading.

We went round to the Great Eastern Hotel, into the
billiard room where Ann had booked seats for the chal-
lenge match between Kingsley Kennerly, the British
Amateur Billiard Champion (now turned pro), & Prince

Hirjee, the All India Amateur Champion. I thoroughly enjoyed the match, the billiards was wonderful. Even Ann was interested to see how the players could make the balls go just where they wanted them.

We stayed until 8 pm, had dinner at a Chinese cafe, & then went back to her place to change into evening dress. The night was really cold, & I wore my stiff shirt for a change. We went by taxi to the Ordnance Club dance, & stayed until 2 am. We never "sat out" a dance, rumbas, quick-steps, tangos, old fashioned waltzes, we got up for them all & at 2 o'clock I was ready for a week in bed.

After taking Ann home, I walked round to the Great Eastern Hotel once more, where Bob & I had booked a room for the night. Now that petrol is rationed, getting back to Dum Dum at night is practically impossible, so we stay most Saturday nights at one of the Calcutta hotels.

In the morning Ann & I came back to Dum Dum. The Club tennis court is now ready for playing, so we spent the afternoon & evening playing tennis & badminton. The Club was crowded with the Dum Dum gang, in the Swimming Pool, on the verandah, playing on the courts or on the billiard table.

Last Thursday Ann & I went to Y.W.C.A. dance in town, & were fortunate enough to win the spot prize, she got a cut glass powder bowl & I won a shaving outfit.

John Beard, the manager of Kodak's of Calcutta, has gone home to England. He has given his black bear to the zoo, & his alsation dog to Bob, & what an animal. Only a year old, it looks like a wolf, eats like a horse, & when in a playful mood, knocks us down & chews our ears. Actually it is a very intelligent & valuable dog. On Sunday when we were all over at the Club, the bearer made sandwiches for tea & left them on the table. "Mike" the Alsation polished off the lot.

I am still as busy as ever arranging dances, the children's Xmas party & a tennis party at the Club around holiday week. Work is plentiful & for once, material is available, so this month we should get back to our normal output.

Bread rationing is very strict. There has been another cut this week, & sugar is to be de-controlled from today, so that means that sugar will just disappear from the market. Coal & fuel is in short supply, the petrol ration is cut to an absolute minimum, & Scotch Whiskey is once more non-existent. However, we don't go short of food; vegetables are plentiful, also fruit, & we can always buy chickens or ducks, & most days fish, while tinned stuff is on the market, although the price is high.

Already there is a lot of dissatisfaction among the workmen with the Indian Government because of the shortage of all commodities; most of the ordinary workers thought that once they got their independence everything would be all beer & skittles.

Pleased to hear that Dad's thumb is almost better; also glad to know that you received all my photographs. About that snap you sent me of the scout patrol up at Upsall (Tommy Brighton & the boys), I already have the original snap, sent to me by Tommy about two years ago, so now I have two of them.

Hope you all have a good time this Xmas, with plenty to eat & drink. We are going to have our bungalow decorated by the girls, & have our Xmas tiffin & dinner in our own place. Every year previously, we have been invited out somewhere on Xmas day, but this year we are going to issue invitations.

After a terrific plague of greenfly, & then mosquitoes, we are now very seldom troubled with insects. I think it is too cold for them. The packs of jackals are round the

compound, howling & barking every night, with all the
pi-dogs in the village joining in the chorus. Best of luck to
all of you & a very merry Xmas. Remember me to all my
friends, Cheerio & love.

Dec. 24th

Christmas Eve, & I am writing this letter in the office. I
haven't had time to sit down during the last week, either
at work or in the evenings.

The Club Dance last Saturday was a huge success & the
Children's Xmas Party was even better on Sunday. About
thirty children were present, & about fifty adults. I was
running the races & had to explain to the smaller kids
what to do in the obstacle races, & as some of the children
were Bengalis, I had to exert all my linguistic abilities in
Hindi & Bengali to explain to them.

The high spot of the day was the old men's race & the
ladies' race. The men, as usual in India, play very rough, &
when the five relay teams of five men each set off, we who
were starting them pushed chairs onto the track, tripped
them up on the corners, & brought them down with
flying rugby tackles. Freddy Brennan crashed through the
tennis screens into the ditch, & Alex Smith had his pants
pulled off. The kids & Bill Howell went wild with delight
at the confusion.

The ladies' race too was just as boisterous, & all the
girls sportingly joined in. I collected all their shoes, tied
them in odd pairs & bundled them up in a sack. The ladies
had to run barefooted to the sack, sort out their own

shoes, & then run the last fifty yards. All the men joined in
to prevent them reaching the winning post & nobody
finished the course.

After tea at 4 pm, we had a Punch & Judy show, & then
Father Xmas arrived. Just like last year, Freddy Brennan
got all dressed up & entered the Club grounds sitting on a
trailer under a garlanded canopy, all drawn by twenty
reindeer (coolies) with a couple of guys banging empty
tins. He distributed presents around the Xmas tree &
after all the kids were tired out & gone home, we finished
up with an impromptu dance in the Club.

This evening we four, Ann & I, & Bob & his girl, are
going to the Ordnance Club Dance in Calcutta. After
staying the night in town, we are coming back to Dum
Dum for Xmas tiffin & dinner. Also Ann's mother will
stay with us until Boxing Day, so we have a house full.
The girls insisted that we decorate the place, so we have
streamers, balloons & what-not draped through all the
rooms. The servants have brought in a large Xmas tree, &
all decorated & lit with concealed green lights, it really
looks wonderful. One of my workmen supplied two
geese for the holidays, so we are all set for some knife &
fork work.

Our programme for the next ten days is full. Jimmy
Bell has invited us to Budge Budge for a New Year's dance
& to spend New Year's day with him. We are expected to
attend a fancy dress dance on New Year's Eve at the
Jessops' Club. We have been invited to dinner at the
Muirs' on Dec. 30th, dinner with the Farrens & Smiths
on Sunday the 28th, Dance at the Club on Saturday the
27th, dinner in Calcutta at the Roberts' on Dec. 29th…
I don't know how we will fit everything in.

Thanks for your Xmas card. I also received one from
Ernie Cooper, one from a certain widow at Normanby,

lots from people in Calcutta, including Evelyn, the girl who stayed at our hotel in Gopalpur, & where we went to the 21st birthday party.

We are as busy as ever at work & our tonnage is up above the 1000 tons mark already this month. There have been odd cases of trouble in Calcutta lately, one where an American was assaulted by a mob in Clive St. when a rumour went round that he had pushed a bearer out of a window. Fortunately, he locked himself with two typists in a strong room, & the arrival of the police prevented the crowd from tearing him to pieces. Also at Howrah yesterday, three jute mills had some trouble with the workmen. European officers & managers were beaten up, & their bungalows & offices were smashed by the mobs because a bonus was not granted by the respective firms. There doesn't seem to be any sense or reason left in India today.

However, as far as I am concerned, I have no worries or grumbles & get the very best out of life, for which I am duly thankful.

Once more, my very best wishes to you-all. Ann says that she has written to you, & incidentally your last letter looked as if it had been kicked from England to India, although the contents were okay. Cheerio.

Love,
Fred

1948

Jan. 7th

Dear Mam,

This letter is actually a request & a chance for you & me to do someone a good turn. Briefly the situation is as follows: Mr. Hickie, our old Storekeeper, a domiciled European of Irish & British stock, has sent his wife & two grown-up daughters to England, where the girls are studying in a Commercial Course. When he attempted through his bank to make them an allowance, his bank refused on the grounds that he & his family, having been born in this country, are technically Indians & have no right to leave.

Mr. Hickie has tried to send money through the firm & through other banks without any success, & he is almost frantic because his wife & daughters are not yet working. Finally, in desperation, he came to me; but I couldn't send any money through my bank, as the permission for the remittance of Sterling has lapsed & cannot be renewed for some time. Mam, if you could possibly arrange to transfer £50 from my money in England to Mrs. Hickie, I & the Hickie family will be very grateful to you.

I hope it is not too troublesome for you, but I think the

bank can easily arrange a Letter of Credit (or draft) to effect the transfer. The Hickies' account is as follows:
Misses Barbara & Margaret Hickie
Lloyd's Bank
Barnstaple
North Devon
Mr. Hickie will give me the equivalent of the £50 in Rupees. So please try to send the money, Mam, & I hope that there is no difficulty for you.

Thanks very much for writing such a friendly letter to Ann. She phoned me from her office as soon as she received it, & came all the way up to Dum Dum on her own last night to show it to me. She was really very pleased. Actually, Ann is the only girl I have been interested in since I left home. She is the type of girl which, these days, is hard to find: a good sport, a good dancer, tennis player, B.Sc. & ex-teacher, she has a really pleasant disposition & a rare sense of humour, & possesses sound common sense.

We had a marvellous time during Xmas & New Years – dances, cinema, parties, tennis, teas. I had not had such a wizard Xmas before in India. At the Ordnance Club on New Year's Eve, we met Jean, the French officer whom we met at Gopalpur, Evelyn, & her two sisters, Yvonne & Vera. We all went round to Jean's place at 3 am, where he stuffed us with paté de foie gras, asparagus, pickled olives & French wines. He took us home in his jeep at about 5 am.

I am finishing this letter off in the office (started during tiffin time) & have just now received your letter posted at Xmas. Note the cuttings enclosed with references to production of English & Scottish shipyards. A magnificent effort, this is the only solution to the high cost of living, & better standard of living all round. More

production & more hard work all over the world, & inflation will disappear. We are getting back to something like
normal, but the lousy Communists are trying to bring the
men out on strike every week. Last Monday was declared
a general strike day throughout Bengal, but Sardar Patel
flew to Calcutta & addressed Calcutta's millions on the
Maidan. Briefly, his main points were, "We have our own
Government now. Carry on working as hard as you can.
We will give you better wages through the medium of
arbitration & not strikes. Do not sabotage the economy
of your own Govt. by going on strike."

The trouble was all caused by a Special Powers Bill
before the Bengal Assembly, whereby the police had more
authority to control strikes, demonstrations of lawlessness. Naturally, the Communists opposed it & caused a
few minor riots in Calcutta to interrupt the Bill's passing.

I am busy as ever. Monday night Lodge, tonight off to
see Ann, tomorrow night badminton tournament at the
Club, & Friday Lodge again. Hope you all keep fit &
happy, & also hope you can help the Hickie family without much trouble.

Jan. 12th

Monday evening, with a thick cold fog outside,
although the bungalow remains warm. This winter I have
felt the cold. I suppose after nearly four years, my blood is
thinning, & I am glad of blankets on my bed at night.
Mosquitoes are numerous & troublesome, but they are
always more of a menace during the cold weather.

Yesterday, Sunday, Ann & I & one of her office friends,

Doreen, borrowed a car from Shalimar Paint Company (where they work) &, accompanied by their head babu, a Bengali Brahmin, set off from Calcutta to visit the Ram Krishna Hindu temple outside of Lillooah. It is a huge building, completed before the war on the Howrah bank of the Hooghly by an American woman, from American money. We had to observe the rules, such as not taking photographs of the temple with anyone standing in front of it (why? I don't know) & we had to leave our shoes outside & walk around the buildings in our stocking feet.

We afterwards visited another very old Hindu temple further up the river. The images & buildings are interesting, but the squalor & filth always kill any enthusiasm that I have in scrounging around these places.

On Saturday evening, Ann & I went to a dance fiesta, in the Monsoon Gardens. Arranged & run by the Parsee community, it was crowded, mostly Parsees & a few Europeans. Ann met several of her old college pals, & very intelligent & attractive these Parsee girls are. There were two dance floors, indoor & outdoor, a cabaret show & a rifle range (.22). Naturally my Home Guard training helped me to score two bulls & two inners, & I collected two quart bottles of Dutch beer, as prizes.

Next Saturday, the different Airways Companies are running a joint dance at the Dum Dum Airport. Everything laid on, & the whole of Jessops' Club are going as one big *happy* (?) crowd. We should have plenty of fun, because Arthur Dwyer, Jock Farren & Co. are always ready to play the fool. Since the Howell girls made their debut at Xmas time, they too, are kicking over the traces, & while their parents look on in disapproval, the girls dance cheek to cheek with all the men and have a real good time.

I don't spend much time in the Club these days, except

at weekends. Through the week I usually go to the cinema one night, one night dancing and one night visiting friends with Ann in Calcutta.

She has certainly taken an interest in our bungalow. Before, it was a typical bachelor residence; now I have a counterpane (or something) on my bed, a cover on my dressing table, shades on the lamps; she has knitted me a pullover, supplied us with a new tablecloth & table mats, taught the bearer & cook how to make pickles. In fact, when she comes up at the weekend, she just takes the place over.

I hope that you were able to transfer the money to Mrs. Hickie without any trouble to yourself; old man Hickie is very grateful.

Work is pretty hard & hum-drum these days, with shortage of efficient staff, & quite a lot of the Anglo-Indian foremen talking about leaving. In fact, two of them are going. Baxter, our Ration Officer, is going back into Jute,& Fuller from Mechanical Works is going to join his family in Bradford. I was talking to Howell the other day about foremen, etc. & he says that they can't get anyone to come out from England.

Several of my men whose homes are on the India-Pakistan border have been taking leave because of communal trouble, & they all speak very seriously about a war with Pakistan. Quite a few of them wish that the British were back here, & in spite of increases in wages, the lot of the working man is a hard one, food & clothing being in very short supply & high in price.

Hope you are all well.

Jan. 20th

The months are rushing away & I am becoming a
grown up man, in years anyway, although I still look
about 22, my body is still hard & strong, & I like to get
around & see & do things rather than think about them.
This year will probably be a decisive one for me, whether
I decide to carry on in India, or make another start in
some other country.

As a matter of fact, about five months ago during the
tail end of the monsoons, when I was feeling lonely & fed
up with riots, trouble & restrictions & for weeks on end
saw only Dum Dum, I decided to 'have a go' in New
Zealand. I got an address from Jock Farren & had already
drafted a letter when I met Ann at our Club one Saturday
night.

I didn't know that there were any young, attractive
girls left in India, unmarried, with a sense of humour &
principles in these days of slack & lax characters. Anyway,
it took me about a week to get to know her (that devastat-
ing charm of mine!!) & the following week we went on
holiday to Gopalpur together, & since then, I have really
enjoyed my leisure time.

She had a good education, being a Bachelor of Science
of Calcutta College, where she did several years as a
teacher before going into the Accounts Dept. of the
Shalimar Paint Company. I taught her how to swim &
improved her tennis & badminton, & she improved my
dancing. We both get a lot of fun from picnics, trips, &
scrounging around temples & old places; & I was
surprised to find that a girl who is such a good sport is

such a capable woman too. She has no servants & does
her own housework & cooking, is an expert at knitting,
plays the piano very well & takes a real interest in our
bungalow, servants, etc.

Well, most of my letters these days contain pages of
Ann, so you will be wondering why I don't marry the girl
(which would be a good idea). In fact, there is only one
point which is difficult, & that is the unwritten law of the
Burra Sahibs & the British Mercantile firms, which says
that "One must not marry a girl born in this country, but
rather find a girl from home!! (England) even if she is a
charwoman's daughter." Never having been to India,
Mam, you cannot realize the class consciousness of the
British who come out here. Although Ann's father was
a Yorkshireman & Burra Sahib of the River Steam
Navigation Company here, her mother was born in
Bangalore of French & British stock who had lived there
for three generations. Anyway, this snobbish business is
rapidly dying out in India these days, especially since we
young fellows of this generation came to work here,
whereas before, most of the assistants were "black sheep"
of wealthy families, sent out to the Empire to redeem
themselves.

The other day I spent in Howell's office, where he told
me that he has given up all thought of going to S. Africa
because of difficulties of getting a passage. Instead he has
booked passages for himself & his family to England for
his six months' leave (so he calls it, although I think that
he might be retiring). He is going to stay in the South,
though he will visit Teeside & promised me that he would
call to see you. The real point of our talk was whether I
intended to sign another contract. Ostensibly he was
asking from personal curiosity, but I suspect that he was
gathering information for the Directors. He was rather

disappointed when I said that I couldn't imagine India would be worth living in after another year, & I thought my future would be more assured in some other part of the British Commonwealth of Nations.

He argued & said that we two lads came out during unsettled & difficult times, which still prevailed; but we had all of the hard knocks of India without any of the beer & skittles. He said that terms of our next contract depended entirely on us. We were now fully competent to run our jobs in technical-assistant-short, Jessop & Co., & if this country settled down, life would be worth living out here once more. There is a lot of truth in what he said, but everything depends on whether India maintains a sensible Government friendly to Britain.

Certainly the present Govt. are working very hard to establish peace & prosperity, & communal harmony. Every day, the big shots emphasize the need for tolerance, harder work, greater production, & the urgent need to suppress all strikes & lawlessness; especially old Gandhi, who is doing a marvellous job in preaching non-violence & the abolition of the caste system. Personally I think that next year when India has the choice of staying in, or leaving the British Empire, Gandhi will prove to be another Jan Smuts & will urge Indians to remain within the Empire. Incidentally, there are many anti-Gandhi Indians these days, when all political Parties are trying to push their ways to the top.

We have had plenty to do in Dum Dum recently. I can't remember the last evening I stayed at home; there is so much to do & no time to write about it. Going backwards, I will mention briefly how I have spent my time.

Last night I left work early, went into town on the motorcycle of one of the foremen. Arriving at Howrah Station at 6 pm, I met Ann & wished her mother a pleas-

ant journey. She left on the Madras Mail for Bangalore
& a holiday with her sister. Ann & I went to the new
Calcutta cinema, "The Society," just opened, & the most
modern cinema I have ever been in. The film was "I
Wonder Who's Kissing Her Now," a good musical show.

Sunday the girls came up from Calcutta & stayed the
day with us. It was warm & sunny, & we played tennis
most of the morning & afternoon at the Club.

Saturday was a really big night. All of the Jessops'
crowd went to a dance at the Dum Dum Airport. Run &
organized by six large Airways Companies, there were
over a thousand people present, two bands & the restaurant was adapted for dancing. In our party was Arthur
Dwyer, Mr. & Mrs. Ewing, Mr. & Mrs. Birchenough,
Mrs. & Maureen Smith, Mr. Doak, Mr. & Mrs. Howell &
two daughters, Tommy Thomson & wife, myself & Ann,
Bob & Doris, Walter Brooks & his pal. I think Saturday
was the first time I had seen Bill Howell in a dress suit.

Friday, Post Office Rd. team played Rajabagan
Compound at badminton at the Club. Thursday, Bob &
I went into Calcutta to a Lodge Meeting followed by a
banquet; here again the Jessops' crowd were well represented & Alex Smith was there too.

The enclosed photograph was taken by Bob, unknown
to me, one Sunday morning at the Club, just as I was
going to crash over a magnificent serve. Actually the ball
seems to be dropping too far in front of me, so this particular serve probably crashed *into* the net.

Today received your letter with newspaper cuttings &
mentioning that you had had my letter telling of Xmas
tamasha. By the way, if you are short of tea, I could probably manage to send you a few parcels. Many people in
U.K. are now asking their friends out here for tea.

Best wishes to all at home.

Jan. 29th

Thanks for arranging for the money transfer to the Misses
Hickie. Mr. Hickie gave me a cheque for the equivalent
amount in rupees, which I promptly spent on an engagement ring. So I am now well & truly caught & will have to
renounce my bachelor life. Actually, I have given the
matter much thought, & being always rather cynical
about marriage, I have made sure that at least nothing will
go wrong with Ann & myself. She is the only girl that I
have ever met that I would consider spending the rest of
my life with, & being as she is a thoroughly sensible &
practical person, we have every chance of making our lives
a success. She is the only girl that I have met who
combines fun & seriousness, work & play, capability with
kind heartedness. She has a great pride in her house, fills
in her spare time knitting, dressmaking, cooking,
rugmaking, & even dabbles in leatherwork. At the same
time she is no stick-in-the-mud, but is a good mixer, good
at sports, a good conversationalist, & shows a lively interest in all subjects. Anyway, I am very fortunate in finding
such a girl, because these days such a person is unique &
impossible to find in India, & possibly in England, too.

As soon as I have had a talk with the Directors & fixed
up about salary, a house, & passages home at the end of
my contract, I hope to get married. Admittedly, I don't
feel very brave about getting "buckled" in church with all
the trimmings, but with Jessops' crowd & the Shalimar
Co. gang, we haven't a chance to keep things quiet, & so I
will have to stand a lot of chaffing & horseplay.

I am sorry that you haven't been able to meet Ann. You

two would get on fine. She has all the qualities which you admire, plays the piano & during the war, played the organ for American troops' church services. Quite frankly, I don't think there is anything she can't do. India these days is no longer a single man's paradise. There is a lot of worry & responsibility attached to work out here now, so someone to look after me, keep me laughing & young is just what I need.

There is some talk of further increases for the imported staff in Jessops, not yet definite, but we expect to receive another 10% of basic pay as an enhanced Dearness Allowance. Also, on top of this, an extra 100 chips a month for the married assistants, which, if we get the extra money, will make us all very comfortably off. Incidentally, the raise is to be back-dated from November, so we should get a lump sum in our next pay.

The weather is very changeable at present, big drops & raises in temperature, which play havoc with one's "tummy." Cholera & Smallpox is rife, & we have all been punctured & vaccinated. My usual colds are very frequent, but not very severe.

Recently Mrs. Howell has been doing a lot of shopping in preparation for going home & very thoughtfully has been buying we two fellows some decent shirting & other materials.

Sat. Jan. 31st

Since starting this letter, Mam, a serious event has taken place in India's history–the assassination of Mahatma Gandhije. Last night, I decided to go into Calcutta after work, & Bob said he would come with me, so at 6 pm we caught a bus to Shambazaar, & then got a taxi into the city where we met Ann & Doris. We noticed crowds of Indians round all the radio shops listening to the news & we wondered what had happened.

The girls told us that Gandhi had been killed, but what 440 million people wanted to know in India was KILLED BY WHOM? Everyone was scared to death that the assassin had been a Muslim, for, if so, the Hindus would have massacred the Muslims & started a real killings. Fortunately, the assailant was a Maratha Hindu & we all breathed again.

Ann & I went round to her friends' place, the Frangopoulos, where we had dinner & listened to the news on the radio. On the way there the Sikh taxi driver was scared to death. He said that Bengalis were assaulting Sikhs & up-country Hindustanis, especially round Shambazaar, which we had to pass on the way back to Dum Dum.

At 10 pm I met Bob & we looked for a taxi with a Muslim driver, just in case the Bengalis & Hindustanis were having trouble. Finding a taxi, we set off, passing through Shambazaar, which was deserted except for carloads of police & military.

Today has been quiet, works, factories, offices, transport, everything shut down. We couldn't even play tennis at the Club, so I have had a lazy day in bed.

The killing of Gandhi is a sign of the times in India. Half the population aren't satisfied even now they have got their Freedom. All the different "jats" & races are pulling, pushing, scheming to fight their way to the top. The Prime Minister of W. Bengal was a Bengali named Ghosh, a non-party man & an able man, an upholder of law & order. He has been pushed out & his job given to another Bengali named Roy. Also the Governor of W. Bengal, Rajagopalacharia, a Madrassi, is not popular with the Bengalis. Gandhi, with his policy of Satyagraha, or non-violence, was a restraining influence on the Indians. So now who can take his place?

For once I have remembered that there are some birth-days at Avonholme, Violet's & Arthur's, round about the 9th & 11th of Feb. My very best wishes to them. Incidentally, Ann's birthday is on Feb. 4th.

Local news is that Joan Farren is definitely returning to India in a month's time. The Howells are going home in April, & our old friend Bury is taking over the manager's job in Structural Works. I don't know whether I mentioned it before, but Howell wants to know whether Bob & I intend to sign a new contract after this five years. We both said that we didn't know.

Best wishes to you all at home, keep fit.

Feb. 9th

Today received your letter in which you mention Gandhi's death; you also mention repercussions. Well, you can see what has happened, the whole plot was a carefully planned scheme to wipe out the present leaders of India. Nehru, Patel & Gandhi stood for a united India with equal rights for all creeds, castes & jats & religions, but the Hindu Mahasabha, & the Rashrriya Swayam-sevak Sangh wanted a Hindu India. Their policy was orthodox Hinduism, with all the castes & customs & a purely Hindu Government. In the subsequent riots the mobs, enraged at the assassination of Mahatmaji Gandhi, smashed offices & assaulted the leaders of the Mahasabha & the R.S.S.S. The Govt. have now outlawed these two parties & have arrested most of the leaders.

On Thursday this week, Gandhi's ashes will be

immersed in the Jumna River, according to Hindu
practise, therefore Thursday is a National Holiday.
Everything will be closed down, Clubs, places of amuse-
ment, transport, so all of India's 440 million will remain
indoors on that day.

This morning a new inspector came in to see me, to
pass a couple of gasometers for the big Sindri Fertilizer
Project. His name is Walton & he comes from Stockton.
He is on loan from Ashmore Benson & Pease for two
years to the Indian Power Gas Co. He has been in this
country ten days & doesn't quite get the idea of things (it
must be pretty astonishing for anyone coming out here
these days). We had a long talk about Stockton &
Middlesbrough, & he was surprised to find Bob & me to
be the only Englishmen running the Structural Works
(Bill Howell has been in Calcutta all day).

I don't know whether I have mentioned it before, but
poor old Bill Howell was arrested in the works the other
day & Baxter, our Food & Ration Shop man, had to go &
bail him out. The trouble arose over some Petrol
Coupons. Bill had used January's coupons on the last day
of December, or some such trifling matter. The Police
checked up on this particular garage & sent a summons to
Bill to attend court. The way the Postal Service works in
this country these days, it is not surprising that the
Summons was never delivered. Anyway, old Bill was
yanked off to the Police Thana, not knowing a thing
about what he had done wrong. That particular day too,
his foot was troubling him & he couldn't walk (he suffers
from some kind of gout & it catches up with him every
year).

Incidentally, when Bill complains about his foot it
always rains, & sure enough, this time it poured down for
three days. The weather is still damp & cold.

Ann has left her cocker spaniel with me. She is on her
own since her mother went for a holiday to Bangalore, &
so when the servant who brings her the dog's meat went
on leave, I had to look after the dog. Now we have the
two animals, Bob's Mike the Alsation, & Meggy the
Cocker. Incidentally, Bob is going to sell Mike to a local
Indian Big-shot for 250 chips.

Bob & I have decided to buy a car. A friend of ours who
works in a large Calcutta garage has selected one for us, &
is bringing it up to Dum Dum tomorrow. Of course the
car is second-hand, but we will save a lot of money buying
it. Between us we spend 300 to 400 rupees a month on
taxis & transport, so if we get a car, we will not have this
expense. The Indian Govt. have relaxed their import
restrictions & so with new cars once more coming onto
the market, the prices of second-hand ones are dropping.

Ann's birthday was last Thursday, so I went into town
to see her. The journey was eventful because the works
bus in which I travelled broke down in pouring rain at
Cossipore. After lifts & short rides in other buses, I
managed to get into the New Market. There I bought
stacks of red roses, absolutely wonderful flowers, filled a
taxi with them & took them round to her place.

She is rather lonely at present, after all it is no fun for a
girl living on her own in a flat, although she has a radio &
her piano. Recently there has been a civet cat in their
compound & several times we have chased it out, after it
had broken milk jugs & crockery looking for food in the
house.

Since starting this letter, I have been over to the Club
where I had a couple of glasses of beer & a game of
snooker with Bill Howell. He told me that he had been in
town all day getting his court case "scrubbed," & after
much trouble, waiting, & visiting several Police stations

(Thanas), he has had his case withdrawn.

The other Sunday Mr. & Mrs. Cargin from our Clive St. Office came up to our Club at Dum Dum for the first time. Mrs. Cargin is almost the best lady player (tennis) in India. She played at Wimbledon with Mehta last year when she was on leave. Her husband is almost in the professional class too, & so we witnessed a real good tennis display with "Birch" & Doak, who are also tip-top players.

This month there is plenty to keep us interested: the Installation Meeting & Banquet at our Lodge, the Masonic Ball at Cossipore Club, the Golf Competition at Tollygunje, which has been put back three weeks because of Gandhi's assassination, a snooker & billiard tournament at Cossipore Club, tennis every weekend at Dum Dum, & if we can get a car fixed up, we can get some decent picnics & outings to places of interest. The enclosed snap was taken by Bob, who did it for Ann. She wanted it to put under her pillow, she says. Frankly, I couldn't imagine anyone wanting to put it under their pillow.

Our 10% increase on basic pay was included in our salary this month, back-dated three months. But recently, the prices of everything have soared, so we need it to keep going as usual.

So far I haven't heard from Vince or Jack Evans, or Tommy Brighton, so I think there is some trouble again with mail deliveries.

Incidentally, I note all your advice in your letter, & have given it the thought it merits. Leave everything to me, I always know the correct road (I hope).

Feb. 17th

Tuesday tiffin time, & with a few minutes to spare, I am
trying to catch up on my letter writing. The weather is hot
& sunny but we haven't yet started to use the fans. In fact,
the nights are extremely cold and damp; this is the last of
the Calcutta winter.

Busy as ever at work, I am equally busy outside of
Jessops. Tonight we have a Club Committee meeting, to
review our year's work. In March we have a General
Meeting & a new committee will take over.

Last Friday was our Lodge Installation Meeting,
followed by a banquet at the Cossipore Club. I met many
people that I hadn't seen for months & had a very interesting evening.

Thursday was the National Holiday, when everything
was shut down because of the Ceremony of immersing
Gandhi's ashes in the several large rivers of India. I spent
the whole day at Ann's flat, where she experimented with
her cooking, I being the guinea pig. Her tiffin & dinner
were excellent, & I thoroughly enjoyed both meals without any bad effects. Ann, of course, was tickled to death
that I polished off all she put in front of me. Most of the
day I drifted around putting a new washer on the tap,
easing a door which was jammed, & fitting bolts &
hinges, etc. Some holiday.

On Saturday we both went to the Ordnance Dance at
Hastings. The British cruiser Birmingham is in Calcutta
Port, so we told the taxi driver to go by the Kidderpore
Road, which runs by the side of the river Hooghly so we
could see the cruiser. It was well worth seeing too, the

night was bright with moonlight & the riverside lights, signals & the portholes of the cruiser all added to the illuminations. The ship looked really marvellous at anchor in the glistening water.

We also passed the India Trades Exhibition in the Eden Gardens. Here again, everything was illuminated. There is a fair included, & although the Exhibition has not been officially opened, all the stalls & buildings are ready & all the machinery & the products to be shown have been installed. I think that Jessops is the only large firm not represented; why, I don't know. Once more the rumours of the firm selling out to Marwaris are circulating.

When Ann & I arrived at the Ordnance dance, men outnumbered the girls by about five to one, because nearly all the Petty Officers of the Birmingham were there. During the tag dances & "gents-excuse-me," I just sat out. It was the easiest way; no sooner had I "tapped" one guy than someone "tapped" me.

On Sunday we had our usual energetic day at the Club. As I was not in tennis kit I couldn't play tennis, so had a couple of games of snooker with the boys, while Ann sat & talked with Mrs. Howell on the verandah about materials, knitting & the usual nonsense (sorry, *sense*). They were so wrapped up in some argument about curtains that the pair of them got into the car & drove round to the Howells' bungalow to settle the argument. Whilst in the house Mrs. Howell told Ann that they are going on six months leave & are definitely returning. While they are in England, they will rent their bungalow to a bachelor; so it seems that they are not leaving India for good.

I am continuing this letter in my office. I have earned a rest today, running around with wagon inspectors, crane inspectors, loading, arguing with the Union, phoning, checking & experimenting. Last night I had decided to

give my beard a rest from shaving, stay in & knock off
a dozen letters, but "the best laid plans of mice & men
gang aft agley." Bob was doing some enlarging of some
portraits we had taken & he wanted me to fix the prints
as he exposed them. Then "Westy" of the Aluminium
Company came in with his daughter & stayed a couple
of hours. Also the tailor turned up. I had sent for him
to measure me for some shirts to be made from the
American disposals materials bought for us by Mrs.
Howell. Therefore my mail remained unwritten.

Ann has just phoned me to say that she has received a
letter from you; I got one yesterday, mentioning peculiar
weather, but it seems to be better than last year at this time.
About Violet's birthday, I did forget the date, but when
someone mentioned that Feb. 14th was St. Valentine's Day
I remembered at once. Ann is making up a parcel for you,
the tea that I promised, & soap & lard (her suggestion).
She has relatives in Bournemouth & the South of England
who are always asking for cooking fats, soap & butter.

Tomorrow evening we are going to a cocktail dance at
the Swimming Club. As far as we are concerned, cocktails
don't enter into it, I might have a couple of beers & Ann
doesn't drink. I haven't yet been to a dance at the
Swimming Club. In fact, I haven't been there at all for
about six months.

Hope you all keep fit & well at home. You don't tell me
much about Arthur's & Violet's activities. I'm afraid that
Ormesby seems very dull to me after the uncertain existence that we lead in India. However, I shall be pleased to
see the old village when I return, with all its new reser-
voirs, etc.

Well, time to pack up now & then over to the Clubhouse for our meeting at 5:30 pm. My best wishes to all &
love.

Mar. 4th

Thursday morning & only 7 am with the sun struggling to shine through the mist, & with hundreds of last night's mosquitoes cruising around. I am not often out of bed at this time of the day, but last night Bob & I had just settled down to a quiet evening of letter writing, when Ann unexpectedly arrived. She left the office at 4:30 pm, went home, stuffed a change of clothes in a bag & came out to see me by bus & taxi. Not a pleasant trip for a girl alone, & about the same distance as Redcar is from Ormesby.[63]

We went for a walk before dinner & called in at the Club, which was deserted because of beer & whiskey shortage. Ann caught the bus back to town at 6:30 this morning. It was quite cold & damp at that time too.

Tiffin time, with a hot, dry wind blowing & about 100° in the sun. The morning passed with the usual labour troubles & disputes. Discipline is practically non-existent, because the foremen, managers, & owners of companies can take no disciplinary action against any man or group of men. The Labour Unions are now so strong that practically nothing can be done without consulting them first. We cannot discharge men for any reason short of killing, so naturally our production is not what it should be. The only solution to this "impasse" is for the present Central Government to realize that, unless some sort of order is maintained, India will never raise her standard of living & will even become bankrupt & face an economic collapse.

Thursday evening, & a *quiet* evening. Bob is making up

a parcel to send home. He has just heard that his girl in Middlesbrough is seriously ill, & so is not feeling very bright. The atmosphere in the bungalow is warm & stuffy, but a breeze is blowing from the jungle, over the tanks & ponds, bringing the scent of the flowering trees & shrubs which are in bloom at this time of the year. Also bringing millions of mosquitoes, which are also in bloom at this time of year.

Bob has just asked me to go around to the Club with him & the dog (Meggy the spaniel), which wants to go for a walk, so once more I shall have to leave this letter.

Monday March 8th
Another weekend gone by with the usual outings & fun. Last Thursday I went into town to see Ann. We visited the New Empire Cinema, where we saw the film "I Will Always Love You," a story of brilliant pianists in America. The music was wonderful, Schumann, Rachmaninoff, Chopin, Brahms, Lizst & Beethoven. Ann probably enjoyed the film more than I did, because she plays the piano herself, mostly classics & ballads.

Friday evening I went to our Lodge of Instruction. Saturday morning at work I finished off an ironing board for Ann, made in our joiners' shop. Since I met her she keeps me going in the works making odd things for her: gadgets for winding wool, gadgets for casting off loops in cable stitch, things for making wool rugs, silk embroidery, fitting handles on two Japanese Hara-Kiri knives for the Burra Sahib in her office, & recently I have been repairing a three-burner cooking stove for her.

On Saturday, Bob & I went into town in the work's station wagon. Bob went on to do some shopping while I went straight round to Ann's place, where I met her mother & her Aunt, who had just returned from

Bangalore. In the evening, Ann & I went to the Ordnance Club dance at Hastings, where I thoroughly enjoyed myself. There was plenty of room for dancing, the night was cool, the band was excellent, I was just in the mood. So we didn't sit out once until we left at 1:30 am to catch a taxi back to her place, where I stayed the night.

Sunday morning we got our usual taxi, picked up Bob & Doris & drove to Dum Dum. Getting changed at our bungalow, we went round to the Club for some tennis. The place was again almost deserted, (no beer or whiskey). Ann & I sloshed the tennis balls about until I was soaked with sweat & roasted by the sun. The heat at midday is terrific, hot & dry.

We cooled off under the verandah fans with a long, cold, orange squash each. The Club grounds are really marvellous at this time, the sunlight on the green water of the swimming pool, the green turf of the tennis court & bowling greens, the hoardes of chattering mynahs in the tops of the cotton trees, the new leaves of the palms, with all the usual Indian birds: the brain-fever bird, the hot weather bird (I think its name is Oriel) & the plonk, plonk, plonk of the coppersmith bird, who is a ventriloquist & can never be seen. The dahlias, cosmos & sweet peas are all flowering too.

The enclosed photograph was taken, developed, printed & toned by Bob. Snapped one Sunday morning on our verandah, it is a real likeness of Ann, & her cocker Meggy. A pity that there was a flaw on the negative, which was an old Belgian film. You can see how we have tried to camouflage with pencil the scratch on her left cheek & eye.

Bob is printing some more films right now, some good ones of the bearer's wife & four of his six kids. Doris had to take the snaps of the bearer's wife, as she wouldn't

come anywhere near us two men. Much Binding in the
Marsh[64] is on the radio, the bearer is fixing the mossie net
on my bed, & Meggy the cocker is chasing lizards on the
wall.

Hope you are all fit & well at home. I read Violet's *short*
letter with interest; her literary efforts evidently rely on
quality rather than quantity. Regards to the Admiral, &
Love.

Mar. 29th

Just received your letter of March 21st with enclosed
Easter greetings card. In this country, Europeans wish
each other a "Happy Easter" as we do at Xmas time
("Merry Xmas, etc."). Strange, that as you received the
photograph of Ann, Auntie Rose should visit you. I don't
know whether you notice any resemblance, but I think
they are very much alike, & their natures are similar too,
from what I remember of Rose.

Today, Monday, we are back at work after the Easter
Holidays, although our Head Office & most of the Clive
Street firms are closed today. Last Thursday, Doljatra
Puja, or Hindu Holi Festival, was a day of complete
hooliganism in Calcutta. This Puja has an unpleasant
origin & is directed against women. It is celebrated by the
lower caste Hindus, who daub, smear & throw paint,
coloured powder & water on each other or any unfortu-
nate Indian women who may be out-of-doors. This year
Anglo-Indian, European & British women, & in some
cases men, seemed to be the targets for the mobs.

I was in town, having slept Wednesday night at Ann's home. On Thursday morning we caught a taxi & drove round to the Metro Cinema to book seats for Saturday. As we came to a halt outside of the cinema in Chowringhee (European shopping centre), gangs of ruffians, smeared from head to foot in paint, poured out of trams running from the low class districts. They had travelled without tickets & the trams were covered with coloured water, drivers & conductors too. Even police who attempted to interfere were daubed & drenched with paint. From the taxi, although I didn't see any Europeans molested, I saw several respectable Indians roughly handled by these gangs of madmen.

After picking up Bob & Doris, we set off for Dum Dum, & unfortunately, our taxi had a front window missing. The roads were lined with gangs of hooligans armed with buckets of red, blue, green & yellow dyes, & syringes and pumps. Any car which stopped, had the doors wrenched open, while the occupants were drenched from syringes with paint.

Fortunately, the old Sikh driving our taxi didn't stop, while I held a piece of cloth over the open window. The outside of the car was drenched time & time again, & the paint, which did get onto our shirts & the girls' dresses, was bleached off by Bob with his developing chemicals. The Doaks weren't so fortunate, & Mrs. Doak had a suit ruined when they were driving in to the Swimming Club. However, at Dum Dum the Indians seemed to be more civilized & there were no hectic demonstrations. We spent the day swimming & playing tennis at the Club. Friday also we spent in Dum Dum, having a lazy time & going back to Calcutta in the evening by taxi. Bob & I stayed the night in town; next morning I was awake early & when Ann went to the office at 9 am (she had to work until tiffin time), I stayed in her flat, fixing a leaky cistern,& doing a couple of odd jobs.

Bob called for me at 10:30 & we went round to the Calcutta Swimming Club. I thoroughly enjoyed the morning there; although I haven't been for several months I knew dozens of people. The outside pool is large enough to have a real swim, the sun was hot & pleasant & the beer was good.

I left at noon to pick up Ann at her office, & what a comfortable office it is, a large nicely furnished room, desk, complete with buzzers, telephone, & calculating machine. From there, we went on to do some shopping in the new market, back to her place for tiffin, then 3 pm show at the Metro, a very interesting film, "Green Dolphin Street." After tea at Firpos we went back to her place, changed, & set off for the Easter Dance at the Ordnance Club.

All our travelling is done by taxi, & the city of Calcutta, being a rambling place, certainly takes a lot of my money in taxi fares. However, we have been promised a car by the Directors for next month, when E.B. Wilson goes home on leave; he is using this car at present to get him into the office.

The Ordnance Dance was the usual entertaining & friendly show, but when we came out at 12:30 there wasn't a taxi to be found, so we had to walk a mile, do another mile & a half by rickshaw, finally getting a taxi to take us the last two miles back to Ann's home.

Sunday morning was rather eventful because I went to church, to St. Andrews' Scots Kirk. I rather like this church, there is no altar or la-de-da, & there are twelve Elders (representing the apostles, I think Judas Iscariot was missing) who very kindly distribute Communion to the congregation where they sit. This is the first time that

I have seen this done. The Easter bonnets of the mem sahibs were awesome in their splendour, from the ridiculous to the sublime. Nothing even slightly resembled a hat. Ann was wearing a piece of round black straw with net & ribbons & elastic perched bang on the top of her head, & as the morning was very hot, she had her hair bang on top too. It looked silly but attractive.

Now for the local news. Joan Farren is expected to land at Bombay on April 2nd, Jock has flown there to meet her. Alex Smith, wife & daughter Maureen, have left Dum Dum to live with the Thomsons at Cossipore. Birchenough is ill in bed with fever. Howell is now saying that he might not go on leave until next year, because the only shipping accommodation offered him & his family was 2nd class in August. I don't know whether I mentioned it before, but the Golf Tournament (Jardine Cup) was a hectic affair. Bob won the wooden spoon for going round the course with the highest number of points. Coming home Arthur Dwyer (drunk), & Bill Howell (also) & Sheila & Joan Howell (sober) in Arthur's car, ran into a tram. Very little damage, however, they had to go to the Police Station. But everything seems to have cleared up. The W. Bengal Govt. have declared the Communist Party illegal & have arrested all the leaders. As most of the Trade Unions were Communist dominated, the banning of the Party will contribute to getting back to normal. Best wishes & Love.

[Included in this letter, a clipping from the paper with four letters to the editor complaining about the behaviour on Doljatra Puja.]

April 19th

Today received your letter of Apr. 12th, but still no
mention of having received your food parcel; it should
have arrived by now. Anyway, when it does turn up, let
me know if the contents are useful. I read with interest of
the Jackdaws in the garden, & also that my god-daughter
will be three years young on May 22nd. I shall remember
to write, although Derek & Rita haven't answered my last
three letters. I suppose they still live at the same address,
"Risca House"?

Tonight I am staying in the bungalow. Bob is out at the
Jessops' Club Committee Meeting; fortunately we have
both left that Committee. Also Bill Howell has been
replaced as Chairman by Mr. Doak, our year of office
having been completed. Bob went along tonight to hand
over the books to the new Secretary, Arthur Dwyer.

Joan Farren has returned from England. She looks very
fit & well, & as usual, joins in the fun in the swimming
pool.

Tonight we have had a storm which has cleared the air
& cooled down the atmosphere. During the day the heat
is terrific.

I could use a secretary to help with my correspondence.
I have just filled in my income tax forms, still written in
English, Clive Street still referred to as Clive Street &
India referred to as British India. Also I have written a
letter to my Bank, another to European Association & a
third to Jessops' Secretary, all this writing having "ganged
up" on me because I spend such a lot of time in Calcutta
with Ann.

Once more the going is pretty tough trying to get some work out of the men; the bone of contention this time being a reduction (for them) in Dearness Allowance. The local Labour Board have a system of paying Dearness Allowance in ratio to fluctuations in the market. The Jagatdal Report is compiled by Govt. experts who …

[Pages 3 and 6 (back to back) are missing from this letter.]

Page 4
…keep out of the heat. Snap No. 2 is one of me on the raft at the Calcutta Swimming Club; not very clear. Bob took it from about 25 yards & had to enlarge it quite a lot. No. 3 was taken from the works' car one Saturday afternoon as we were going into town. This Hindu temple is very old, & therefore could not be moved, so the road had to be built around it. As the road at this point is wide & straight, the temple forms a dangerous obstacle in the path of speeding traffic. This is the place where Alex Smith had his elbow smashed with a stone, while driving his car back to Dum Dum one night about a year ago.

I have also received an interesting letter from Violet. She certainly seems to have her future all planned, even if it does involve a lot of study.

Pleased to see that you are arranging to take a holiday at Scarboro, although one week seems a very short stay, compared to my usual three weeks anyway.

Having less than a year to complete my contract, I have given a lot of thought to what I should do. So far I have not contacted the Directors about a new contract or about my passage home. I suppose they will take a dim view of my getting married just now. It isn't usual on the first agreement, & they would have to pay me another 300 rupees a month marriage allowance, find me a bungalow & also pay Ann's passage to England when I go on leave. Anyway, the next two months will decide everything one way or the other.

I have no desire to return to England to work, life seems to be dull & austere, with ever increasing restrictions. Personally I am surprised that Britain's young generation aren't emigrating. After all, 48 million people packed into a small island, not even self-supporting, haven't a chance in the world today, & look at the millions of square miles of Canada, South Africa, Australia, New Zealand, etc. which need populating. If the British people spread....

April 26th

Monday night, & after the usual daily round & common task it is a pleasure to have a cold shower & sit around in shorts, with the windows open & the evening breeze blowing from across the maidan.

Life is fairly quiet for us these days, the weather is too hot for wanting to use up any energy; too hot for dancing, & wearing coats & collars & ties is sticky & uncomfortable. Ann said that she has written to you. The other day when I phoned her at her office she told me that as there was an eclipse of the moon that night, all the babus & Indian clerks had taken leave to go & bathe in the Ganges; so as she had nothing to do, she was writing some letters.

There is an epidemic of plague in Calcutta, the same disease which wiped out most of the population of London before the Great fire.

[Pages 2 & 5 (back to back) are missing from this letter.]

Page 3 ...However, this state of affairs didn't suit Ann. "Young man," she said, "You come with me to see a doctor. If you don't eat there must be something wrong; & if I get a husband who is short in height, at least I want him to be broad & solid." Anyway, I took a morning off & visited a Calcutta doctor. He gave me a thorough overhaul; he said that I was an extremely healthy individual but with a frame like mine I could & should carry another two stones of meat. After a couple of tests he pronounced that (as he delicately put it), I had "bugs in the guts", or rather, there were traces of amoeba cysts. So I am on a fifteen day course of dynamite pills to remove the intruders. In this country it is impossible to avoid getting germs in the stomach as all food is more or less contaminated in hot & changeable weather. Still, I continue my work & play without any loss of vigour. Also it is nice to think that someone is firm enough, & thinks enough about me, to keep me toeing the line & healthy.

Page 6 ...manufactured by Nestle's & called Nespray, when mixed with water & iced it is ideal.

Our new Road Roller Shop is now in full swing. We all have had to transfer some men, & as this is the month for marriage among the Hindus, a lot of my workmen have taken leave; hence my labour now numbers 300 instead of the previous 400 men.

Hope you have a good time at Scarboro', but why don't you lash out a bit & have three weeks in Switzerland or at least France? You haven't seen outside of England yet, & don't know that foreigners (as we call them) are usually damned nice people. We have a new foreman in the Mechanical Works, a Hungarian named Vaidja. He &

his wife are very nice people. They are usually at the Club
at weekends & although Vaidja has only one leg, he is a
powerful swimmer.

Hope you & the family (wherever they are scattered)
keep well.

May 7th

Another week & I shall be 28 years old. I don't know
whether "life begins at 40" or 30, but I suspect that it
depends on the circumstances. Just at present, Churchill
is speaking on the radio, & by the sound of his voice, I
would say that he finds life interesting even at 70.
(Incidentally, he is warning us about the Russian
menace.)

Today has been extreme with regard to weather. The
morning was hot & humid (after recent rains); by tiffin
time the heat was almost unbearable; & by 3:30 pm, I was
outside on a crane structure from where I had a wonderful view of the works, the paddy fields, & in the background, the tall palms & the jungle. The atmosphere was
like the inside of a furnace & then came the wind, from
the Nor'East, so we knew we were due for a storm. As the
black clouds appeared on the horizon (they roll up very
quickly in this country) the palm trees were leaning over
in the gale. I don't think anything looks so fine as a gale
over a tropical jungle. Then came the rain, & the downpour has continued since 4 pm. Just at present there is a
real display of fireworks, terrific flashes of lightning, &
thunder which shakes the foundations of the bungalow.

Yesterday was Bob's birthday. We both left work early
& went into town on the foremen's bus. Bob went off
with Doris to the pictures, & I went off with Ann to the
Dentist's. When I visited the doctor two weeks previously, he said that one of the causes of my loss of appetite
was the fact that I had few grinding teeth & therefore
didn't chew my food properly. Anyway, Ann yanked me
off to her dentist, where I had a wax impression taken of
my gums with a view to being fitted out with some false
back teeth.

Ann insisted on coming into the room with me &
while I sat in the chair, she sat on a stool & kept up a
running fire of questions to the dentist: What capacity
were the light bulbs? What sort of wax was it? What were
teeth made of? etc. etc. She is a likeable & friendly girl
with an active mind.

After leaving the dentist's, we did some shopping, &
then had dinner at a Chinese cafe. I met Bob at 10:30 pm
to come back to Dum Dum. The local Government have
once more "axed" the petrol ration, & we find it increasingly difficult to find a taxi to do the Dum Dum trip.

This month I received my usual annual raise. Lumped
with extra Dearness Allowance & Provident Fund contri-
butions, it makes a difference of about 50 chips to my
total income. Ann, too, got a raise bringing her salary up
to about £6 per week by your standards.

Pleased to see that you were pleased to receive the
parcel, & that the cooking fats & soap came in useful. I
shall endeavour to send more parcels in future.

Howell is once more back at work after having all his
teeth out. He tells me that he has been offered a passage
for the end of May, so he might reach England yet this
year. Mr. Doak has been sick with dysentery & is now
recovering in a Nursing Home.

Last weekend was Labour Day, May 1st &, as the Trade
Unions decided to recognize it, Saturday was declared a
holiday & we had to work Sunday morning instead. A
stupid arrangement, as most of the men didn't turn up for
work.

On the night of the first of May there was a dance at the
Club. We hadn't intended going, but at Ann's suggestion,
we left town by taxi at 9 pm & arrived at the dance by 10.
Joan Farren was there. She has changed a lot since she
went home on leave.

Our Road Roller Project is well on the way. The first
one has been completed & has been driven round the
Works. About June, when we have completed several, it is
proposed to have a big Tamasha in the Mechanical Works
with all the Foremen, Jessops' Directors, Managers, all
the big shots from Aveling Barfords Grantham Road
Roller Works, who are flying out specially for the occasion. Also some of the Labour ministers & members of
the Central Indian Government will be there to witness a
"trundle" past of the first Diesel Road Rollers to be manu-
factured in this country. Probably news reel film shots will
be taken, too.

I have almost completed my course of pills & my
appetite has certainly improved. The plague epidemic is
subsiding, being replaced with a cholera epidemic. This
week the local health authorities came into the Works to
innoculate the workmen. We on the staff took a "poke" as
well. Ghastly stuff, by far the worst injection I have had.
The arm becomes very painful, & a high fever follows the
next night, with smarting eyes & a general weakness for
the following two days. After the men had all taken a
"poke" there was very little work done for a couple of
days.

Since starting this letter I have received yours of the

2nd of May, telling of Arthur's trip to London & beyond.
You must get pretty lonely with two of us away, but as
long as we keep writing & coming home, at least every
three years or so, it isn't so bad. Look after yourself and
have a good time. Ann told me today that she had sent a
Babu down to the Export Office to see if she could get a
licence to send you five pounds of cooking fat. I hope she
is successful.

All the best wishes for your health & happiness.

May 26th

Tuesday evening & I have pulled a chair and table out on
to the verandah to write this letter. Although only 6 pm, it
is almost dark, the first bats are flying around; the sky is
blue but hazy & the atmosphere steamy & still.

Looking down into the compound I can see the
bananas in bunches on the trees, & next to our bearer's
godown is a huge mango tree with the fruit almost ripe,
& next to that a small pomilo tree, absolutely laden.
During a recent Nor' Easter storm, two of our papaya
trees were blown down, also several large trees in the
vicinity.

Now, to dispel any fears about the state of my health, I
have finished with the doctor. I have not been absent
from work, and I eat as well as possible with the temperature between 95° & 100°. My only worry was that my
weight went down to ten stones, & my appetite wasn't
very keen, although I felt fit enough.

Therefore don't worry about my health, I am too

wicked to die young, anyway Ann wouldn't let me. The other night I used the public phone in the c.p.o. & when we got back to her flat she made me wash my ear with Dettol, just in case. I would never have thought about the danger of infection.

I still haven't had any official reply from the Directors to my application for a house & the usual amenities available to married overseas employees, although verbally Mr. Sitwell, the Works' Director, stated that everything would be fixed up without any trouble.

The mosquitoes have now arrived in force with the darkness, so I shall "paddle off" to the Club with the dog for a beer & a game of snooker with the boys (the dog doesn't drink), until dinner time.

May 31st

Almost a week since I started this letter & since May 26th the weather has become progressively hotter & steamier. At midday it is now 102° to 104° *in the shade,* with outside temperatures of 110°. Fortunately I have something to do all the time, my mind is occupied every minute. In fact, that is why I am so late in completing this letter.

On Saturday I went into town with Bob in the Works Studebaker car. After dropping Bob at the Swimming Club, I picked up Ann & we went round to the warehouse of Turner Morrison's (where she works). We had bought two Frigidaires for 500 chips (£37-10s) & stored them in the firm's godown until I could arrange transport. I had a mistry & three cookes with me, so we loaded the Frig's onto the Studebaker & sent them off to Dum Dum. Now I am studying Refrigeration Engineering so that I can get them into proper working order. Ann has supplied the paint, so we intend to keep the best one for ourselves & sell the other. We should get about 700 rupees for it.

After loading up the Studebaker, we called in at a furniture store & bought some other items, had tea at a Swiss cafe, & then walked round to the Swimming Club to see if there was to be a dance that night. After dinner at our usual Chinese Restaurant (I like my Chicken Chow Mein), we went back to Ann's place & changed into evening dress. Arriving at the Swimming Club at 10:30 the dance was in full swing; the dancing was on the long verandah, but we sat out under a canopy by the side of the outdoor pool.

I wish you could have been there just to see the moon, & the reflection of the coloured lights on the glistening water, with a crowded verandah, old looks, new looks, most of the women in a sort of three-quarter length evening dress with voluminous skirts & ballet shoes (Ann says that this is now the height of fashion; I call it the height of ruddy nonsense). Anyway, I thoroughly enjoyed it. From the verandah we could see a few swimmers on the diving boards in the inside pool. The splash of the water helped psychologically to offset the heat.

Incidentally, the atmosphere was terrifically humid. Most of the men (I was among the first) took off their tuxedos & dinner jackets, & at least when sitting out, we caught what little breeze there was from the water. Mr. & Mrs. Jean McIntosh were there; they have been in India for three weeks since returning from Ireland. In case you forget, I stayed at their cottage at Singamari Darjeeling. By the way, Birch is flying to Darjeeling tomorrow; Alice is already there, & Mr. & Mrs. Doak too, Mr. Doak recuperating from dysentery.

Today, received a letter from you & also one from Ernie Cooper. Thanks for your enclosed booklet on leathercraft. I am sure Ann will appreciate it, although she knows most of the fundamentals.

Yesterday, Sunday, we were at Dum Dum all day, Ann & I swimming in the morning. We both got well & truly sunburnt, even while in the water. Ann was thrilled to bits, because I had bought her a new swimming costume, a real smasher, made in Switzerland & expensive; but she gave me such a nice set of cufflinks for my birthday that I had to get her something.

On Sunday evening we sat by the side of the Pool under the palms & I demolished two long, cool, crisp, sparkling amber beers; these are the best parts of life in India after the heat of the day.

This month our output has increased slightly in the Works, but material supply & Labour troubles still make our work into hard work. We still live in hopes of getting a bonus, I could put the money to very good use. Bob has had a little six weeks old black cocker pup given him, so once more we have two dogs in the house. This week I have a Lodge meeting, plenty of homework on the Frigidaires, & will drift into town to see Ann twice through the week. Hope all the scattered Clan "Trunbrock" are all well & happy.

June 17

The monsoon is now three days old, & we have had rain
with intervals of showers since the first thunderstorm
started. However, the wind & rain breaks the long spell of
heat we endured early this month. Sunday was just about
the hottest day this year. The Jessops' Club swimming
pool was crammed in the morning, everyone smothered
in prickly heat. Even little Ian, Joan & Jock Farrens' child,
was covered with heat rash, although he didn't seem to
mind as he splashed around in the pool on Jock's shoulders.

While I remember, I will thank you for the book you
sent on leatherwork. Ann says that it has some useful
hints which she did not know. Anyway, she appreciates it
very much.

I don't think I mentioned it previously, but as I had
had no reply from the Directors to my application for a
bungalow, I tackled Mr. Bury, our acting manager, &
asked for an interview. He fixed up for me to meet Mr.
Sitwell, the Works' Director, on Friday. So after tiffin, I
spruced myself up & drove in to Clive St. in the Works'
car.

The interview lasted for two hours. Sitwell hummed &
hawed, sucked his pipe, frowned, smiled – in fact, he tried
to discourage me from getting married. Actually his argument was pretty sound. He stressed the fact that I had
been away from home for over four years, tucked away in
the jungle without very much chance of meeting people,
& well, frankly, he thought that Ann had had no competition. He suggested that I waited until I had been on leave,

met my old friends, & renewed my contact with England
& home. I replied that, as 28 years was a critical age, I
would (deducting one month for travel) during my five
months in England probably land myself with some
female so & so that I hadn't had time to really get to know.
On the other hand, I have known Ann for ten months,
have been on leave with her & intend to marry her.

Eventually Sitwell said, "Okay, you win. If I told you
the Company could not grant you permission, you would
resign, & we don't want you to resign. So go ahead."

As a matter of fact, I had made up my mind to resign if
Jessops refused to allow me to marry on my first contract,
& had made a few enquiries about another job. However,
everything is now settled, so in four to six weeks, I should
be "buckled." Howell of course thinks that I should wait
until I go on leave too, but I am not interested in what
anyone else says or thinks. I do just as I want to do.

Last night I went into town to see Ann, although the
rain did not ease off. We were fortunate in getting taxis, &
so we didn't get wet. We went to the New Empire to see
Margaret Lockwood in "The White Unicorn," a story
with depth & some good acting; in fact, a first class
British Production. Coming home at midnight with my
usual old Sikh taxi wallah, we almost got stranded in
floods on the way.

Dum Dum news: Birch & Alice & Mr. & Mrs. Doak all
flew back from Darjeeling yesterday, completely restored
to health, but all completely broke. Howells' boat has
been put back a month, so he expects to sail in July (about
the 20th) The Ewings are going home in August for six
month's leave. Sitwell suggested that I take over their
bungalow while they are away, but I am not very keen, as
I will have to shift once more when they return.

We have another Yorkshireman in Dum Dum, named

Hayward. I met him when he joined our Lodge. He comes from Bradford & has just left the Bengal Police, & now works in the Gramophone Company here.

Recently I have seen quite a lot of snakes. They come out of holes when the rains come. On Monday my men killed a Russell's viper on my inspection bench. Yesterday evening we killed a house krait on the wall dividing the mens' showers in the Club. On Wed. last we killed a common krait in the Drilling Dept. All three snakes are among the most dangerous in India.

According to today's news there will be some trouble over Hyderabad. The India Govt. have declared an economic blockade of the Nizams' domains, so this means trouble.[65]

We are still struggling along in Jessops with our Labour troubles & low output, although we have about 20 year's work in hand. We did not get our bonus last month, although I understand that it has been sanctioned by the Directors. It seems they have no ready cash to pay out. The Company is financially sound on paper, but no one seems to pay their bills these days, including the Indian Govt. & the Railways. No one seems to know whether India & Pakistan will remain in the British Commonwealth. Personally, I think they will. The present Governor of Bengal (West), Rajaji, Rajagopalacharia to you, is to take over from Mountbatten this month, or next. Rajaji is a good man, I believe he is a South Indian.

You never tell me in your letters whether England is back to normal yet. I read of many troubles in the papers, but how does it affect you personally?

The recent Test match with the Australians provided some interesting listening for us on the radio. We can pick up some good programmes from here.

Hope you all keep fit & are enjoying the English summer. I am pleased to hear Arthur likes his new job, & see that Dad still spends all his time either at Cargo Fleet or at meetings. Best wishes to you all; see you in less than a year.

June 29th

I just can't find time for letter writing. We are so busy at work & I have so much to do, polishing furniture, repairing the Frigidaires, Lodge meetings, trips into town to see Ann. I am writing this effort at the tiffin table. Outside the rain has started again, typical monsoon weather, showers, bright intervals, occasional heavy storms, & sometimes two or three days of drizzle with variable temperatures.

Just before I left work today a delegation of Structural apprentices came to see me, requesting that Bob & I run a sort of night school after work two nights a week, so that they can learn the trade. I would like to help them, but at present I'm afraid my hands are full.

Jessop & Co. have their hands full of trouble too, with the Wagon Works shut down & the Foundry on strike. The Foundry is Jock Farren's pigeon. The trouble started when Jock refused to allow a man to leave the works. The man had received information that his wife was sick, so he told the Union & the shop shut down. Jock has no tact & cannot speak Hindustani, so is very badly liked by the men.

The Wagon Works trouble was due to bad management by the Directors. A new electric plant had to be installed so the power had to be shut off for Saturday morning &

Monday. The men were informed not to come to work, but they demanded pay for the duration of the shut down. Management refused & took out the men's time cards from the racks. The Union told the men to report for work, & if their cards were not in the racks, to go & sit by their benches & machines.

The power is still shut off & will be off until Thursday, but every day the men turn up & sit in the Workshops. The question has now been taken up by the Labour Tribunal & I think Jessops will have to pay the men half-pay for the duration of the stoppage.

On Saturday afternoon, all Jessop's employees attended a Union meeting held on the maidan next to our bungalow. I heard some of the debates & there was a lot of talk of beating up Jock Farren. Eventually they decided to ask for his metallurgist Roy's (Bengali) discharge from the Company. Now the decision rests with the Directors.

Ann & I & Bob had tiffin at the Farrens' house on Sunday, so we heard Jock's version of the story. The Farrens' child Ian is a fine kid. He will be one year old next month, & is very intelligent for his age.

Mr. Howell has not yet left. He has been ill in bed for the past week, so I have not seen him or his family. I understand that they are sailing on the second of next month.

Now for a delicate subject. All this purchasing of furniture & preparing for starting married life has left me with only a slender balance in the bank. I had not bargained for wanting to start a home in this country, that is why I transferred my surplus capital to England. Also I hoped to get the bonus three months ago, which so far has not materialized. Have I any money in a bank account in my name, Mam, I would like to transfer about £50 or £75 to my bank out here. If the money is in your name I won't bother, because Ann has a little money in the bank which we can use. Last month Bob, who was in deep financial difficulties, wrote to his bank in Middlesbrough asking them to send him 500 rupees, which they did without any trouble. Don't get the idea that I am bankrupt, far from it. After all, not many people start off with a house fully & well furnished, which is what I intend to do, radio, piano, in fact, everything, including a Frig. Anyway Mam, if it is at all possible, I would like to have £50, but on no account must you put yourself to any trouble, or take money from your account, or mess around with forms & statements.

Recently I have received a number of letters from you since you returned from Scarbro'. I am pleased that you enjoyed yourself, but also am surprised that you only had one week. One of the letters you sent had unfortunately been damaged in the post, or had been deliberately cut open. It had four shilling stamps attached, so some of the contents were missing. Enclosed was a booklet of views of Scarboro' but no letter or anything else. I hope it wasn't important. I was also pleased to hear that "Skute" remembered me. Give her my love, well – you had better just give her my regards now.

On July 31st I am hoping to get married & then to go for two weeks to Gopalpur, however the Directors are still playing the fool, & although I have verbal permission, I still have not got anything in writing.

We have completed six Road Rollers in our new Road Roller Shop & expect to have the official opening this next month with Pandit Nehru & the big shots down. Incidentally, there is a detachment of police at each works' main gates these days, just in case any trouble starts over the Foundry & Wagon Works incidents. Let's hope that we haven't a strike on our hands when Nehru is scheduled to come.

I am off into town tonight to see Ann, have dinner &

go to a picture show. I have just selected some cloth &
have been measured for a new suit at Ann's instigation.
She says she is not going to marry anyone looking like a
tramp. Anyway I have seen some handsome tramps, so
what?

Hope all the family keep fit, well & happy, even if the
Australians are hammering us & Mannion is leaving the
Boro.

July 6th

Just at present I don't know whether I am on foot or on
horseback, I have so many things to do. The Works'
Director, after much prodding from me, has finally come
across with permission in writing. Therefore, Ann & I
will be well & truly married at 3:30 pm on Saturday July
31st at the Scot's Kirk (St. Andrews). They tell me that the
service only lasts twenty minutes, but they tie the knot
extremely tight. Anyway I have been fixing up Frigidaires,
French polishing furniture, getting the downstairs flat of
No. 10 Post Office Road cleaned up, repaired & painted,
cutting the jungle from the compound, buying railway
tickets, fixing up accommodation at Gopalpur, getting
measured for a new suit, hunting for crockery & cutlery,
looking around for a ring, fixing up transport for the big
day, studying in between for my job in the Lodge &
trying to carry on as usual at work.

Jessop's head designer, E.B. Wilson, has become very
ill with cancer of the throat in England & will not return
to India. His furniture is to be publicly auctioned,

although any of Jessop's staff will receive a 20% discount
on anything they may purchase. I have made a few
preliminary bids for several items.

Mr. Sitwell asked me to take my leave from next July so
that Bob & I are not on leave together; therefore I have to
book my passage now & arrange for passports, etc. By
next month I should be quite distinguished looking with
a fine head of grey hair.

After Ann insisting, & well all the boys expect it of me,
we will have to invite most of Jessop & Co. & half of
Turner Morrisons' to the wedding. Fixing up the reception will be a tough job for me, & I shall have to go hunting for booze & cups & plates, etc. I suppose that any of
the Compound mem-sahibs would help me but they
would want to splash the rupees around & have a big bust
up. Therefore, in the interests of economy, I must do it
myself because I am hard up at present. If you can manage
to transfer a little money to me, Mam, I would be
extremely grateful & it would make an ideal wedding
present. Not that I am broke normally, but everything is
so expensive at present, & getting married & starting a
home is a big item in any country.

Incidentally, Bob will be my best man. The Howells
will not be there, as they are leaving shortly, also the
Ewings sail on July 28th, so they too will be absent. Ann's
burra sahib, Stephens, has agreed to give her away, so all
the participants at the battle have been arranged.

Ann & I are going to Gopalpur for two weeks' holiday
& brother!!! do I need it.

July 9th
Friday & another attempt at your letter. Since starting
it I have been into town again on Wednesday evening
scrounging round all the shops for curtain material. As

curtains run at three to four chips a yard I was hoping we wouldn't find any. Women, when shopping, are the most contrary animals. First of all we must find a neutral colour, & not knowing what a neutral colour was, I kept silent. Therefore, Ann says, "Why don't you say something? Aren't you interested? Tell me what you would choose." So I timidly pointed out a nice quiet grey (at least I thought so), but Ann laughed me to scorn, so I once more relapsed into silence. Eventually, after opening every roll of fabric in the shop, she narrowed down the issue to two shades, & I was requested to select one. As soon as I picked the dark cream, she promptly bought the other.

To give you some idea of what is happening in this country compared to the old days, I am enclosing a typed poem with English translations of the Hindi.

Just recently a Board of Arbitrators have been sitting in Calcutta to establish some sort of arrangement for basic pay, holidays, benefits, & discharging of unwanted manual workers. When these new rules come into force the Indian workman will be better off than his European counterparts. He will get a regular ten days' paid holiday, fifteen days' casual leave, & eight days' paid festival holidays. He also usually takes another month to go to his village up-country. The Board have recommended a month's bonus, or production bonus on output. The workman cannot be retrenched & even if he commits an offence, he must be informed in writing to give him a chance to defend himself when his case comes up before the Union or Tribunal.

Many of my men coming back from the U.P. from leave say that the weather there is terrific. The hot "Loo" winds are killing off many people, while sun temperatures are around 125° every day. Cholera, plague & smallpox are taking a heavy toll of the rural population. Their monsoon will not break until the back end of July. Our monsoons are in full swing, showers every day, roads & drains flooded, leaking roofs, moulding clothes, &, worst of all, damp cigarettes; it is impossible to get a decent smoke.

I believe Ann wrote to you last Monday, so you will already know the date when you receive my letter. Ann says that her office is in utter confusion, everyone is deciding who is going to sing, what they are going to wear, etc. etc. etc.

Well, Mam, best wishes to all at home, & explain to Ernie Cooper how busy I am.

THE BURRAH SAHIBS' LAMENT.
or
TIME MARCHES ON.

We represent the Burrah Sahibs who live in West Bengal,
And frankly now we do not like the look of things at all,
In fact it takes us all our time to summon strength to call
    BEARER, CHAR CHOTA PEG LAO:[66]

In days gone by our income we could reckon by the
    crore,[67]
We'd lots of cars and horses too and servants by the score,
But super tax today has brought starvation to our door!
    BEARER, CHAR CHOTA PEG LAO:

For thirty years from ten to four we bravely bore the load,
Of daily toil in Clive Street, widely famed as our abode,
But now you'll find us working in Netaji Subhas Road!
    BEARER, CHAR CHOTA PEG LAO:

There was a time when office clerks were really most
   polite,
No matter how we cursed and swore the Sahib was
   always right,
But now they tell us what to do and lock us in all night!
      BEARER, CHAR CHOTA PEG LAO:

The joys of Railway trips in Hindusthan have not
   increased
The carriages have had no lights for three years not at
   least,
Whilst the bathrooms hold the secret of 'The Perfume of
   the East'!
      BEARER, CHAR CHOTA PEG LAO:

Of the menus at the Bengal Club we proudly used to boast,
Six courses every night we ate including fish and roast,
But now its just one 'A' two 'B' and one thin piece of
   toast![68]
      BEARER, CHAR CHOTA PEG LAO:

At Christmas out to Belvedere we proudly drove by car,
In state to dine with vintage wine and lots of caviare,
But now we're asked to Government House and given
   cups of chae![69]
      BEARER, CHAR CHOTA PEG LAO:

The present price of Whiskey brings a crisis we must face,
We either give up drinking or court ruin and disgrace
To suggest we'd shirk the issue is an insult to our race!
      BEARER, CHAR CHOTA PEG LAO:

In fruitless search for flats to let with rage we near
   explode,

The Government have commandeered each possible
  abode,
Till the only vacant homes today are in Karaya Road!
  BEARER, CHAR CHOTA PEG LAO:

The thought of what we suffered during War time makes
  us boil,
Those petrol cuts, no beer at all, those extra hours of toil,
Not to mention Yanks and Popsies in the bunkers at the
  Royal![70]
  BEARER, CHAR CHOTA PEG LAO:

To sum it up, we clearly see the writings on the wall,
With prohibition coming we don't want to live at all,
For who would be a Burrah Sahib if not allowed to call
  BEARER, CHAR CHOTA PEG LAO!

July 26th

Just time to scribble a few lines in between rushing
around. The reception is not to be held at 10 Post Office
Road now; one of Shalimar's Directors, Mr. Woolford,
has gone on leave to England, & his house is being occupied by a couple of young Oxford fellows who work for
Turner Morrisons. One of them named Cooke asked Ann
if she would like the use of the house. She jumped at the
chance, hence the reception is to be at Alipore, the really
snooty end of Calcutta. Most of her Directors & big shots
are coming & their wives are helping with food, etc.

Some of Shalimar's chaps & all of Jessops' gang are
searching for whiskey, almost unobtainable in Calcutta
recently. About 60 people are expected to attend, including Jessops' Works' Director & his wife, Mr. & Mrs.
Sitwell, Mr. Bury, our manager, the Doaks, the Birches,
the Farrens, Bill & Jean Muir, Freddy Brennan, Jack
Devereaux, Wally Brooks, & me.

Bob told me (it's a secret, actually) that our Dum Dum
Lodge is buying us a present, fortunately I have invited
the Master to attend. We have already received a lot of
presents: walnut carved book-ends, silver coffee spoons,
Indian carved wood ivory inlaid tray & cigarette box, a
silver cigarette case for me, an electric iron, a set of hand-
painted glassware from Mr. Chang, the head of the Hong
Kong or Shanghai Bank, a cheque for 50 chips. Ann & I
were rather disturbed when you mentioned sending us
linen or something for which you would have to give up
your valuable coupons. After all, we would appreciate
very much any little thing you cared to send, but we
would not like you to do without anything to buy us a
present, as we live in the land of plenty. We will be home
next year & you can buy us something then.

I received a letter from Arthur (spelled phonetically).
He was glad to hear that I had found a "feamail" who
would have me. Also in the same mail was a letter from
Ernie Cooper. I see from your last letter that he has had
the offer of a much better job. I hope he takes it. I always
told Ernie that he was "exploited."

The downstairs flat is almost ready for moving in the
furniture. I have had painters & electricians in all the
week, colour washing the walls & fixing things up in
general. Anyway most of the arrangements have been
made & we are all set. If you see Ernie Cooper, explain to
him that I haven't much time for writing, but Ann should

be able to tell a good tale to his wife Ethel after a while. They are both ex-schoolmistresses.

Best wishes to all the family, & love,

Aug. 25th

The first real opportunity I have had for a month to write you a long letter. Even now I seem to be as busy as ever with work & looking after the house, garden, servants, etc.

As I told you previously I am living alone in Dum Dum. Ann was pretty ill the day we were married & at Gopalpur. She had fever, cold, cough, sore throat, & a general tiredness after all the rushing about for the wedding. The difference the sea air made to her health was amazing & knowing that Calcutta is a particularly lousy place at this time of the year, & at the suggestion of the doctor who had a look at her at Gopalpur, I left her by the seaside for another two weeks. It was against both our wishes, but we felt that if she regained her health completely, the sacrifice was well worth it.

Ann is coming back home on Saturday the 28th, so we have got the worst over, & she says she is very fit. She hasn't missed a day writing to me, in fact sometimes she writes twice a day & I, of course, answer them all.

While I have been on my own I have put a lot of hard work into the bungalow, but at least I have realized an ambition of my life: I can open the Frig. door, & there before me are eggs, fresh milk, iced beer, cold chicken, fresh meat, pears & peaches (they taste so good with a crisp frost on them), butter, tomatoes & fresh vegetables. Everything is mine, no rents or hire purchase to pay. I like to feel that I am entirely independent.

The drawing room: a huge room with ten double doors, most of them leading out onto the verandah, furnished with a three piece suite, settee & two roomy chairs, piano & stool, contra table, a large standard lamp. Actually we need a little more furniture here, but everything belongs to us completely.

The bedroom has my dressing table, Ann's dressing table, two beds, two almirahs (wardrobes), my writing desk, (which belongs to Jessops, but I borrowed it), two chairs & stool. The attached bathroom has a washbasin but no bath, only a zinc tub. I am going to build in a bath & tile it myself. There is a shower & a dressing table which Peter Page & I pinched one night from the old B.D.O. building.

The dining room has a huge dining table, "dooley" (a sort of wooden pantry with gauze sides to keep out insects), a large sideboard, a tea trolley, the Frig. & three chairs I borrowed (?) from the chummery. The large room at the end contains a linen cupboard in which we store tinned food & cutlery, crockery, etc. (Ann's own), kerosene, three burner cooking stove & oven, & a camp bed, suitcases, badminton & tennis rackets. Attached to this room is also a fully equipped bathroom.

Outside is the bawarchi khana or kitchen which is used by our cook. I have started three new servants: a full time cook on 50 rupees a month (he is a Christian), a full time Muslim bearer on 45 rupees a month, & a full time sweeper on 40 rupees a month. The "mali" (gardener) is on the Works' books & comes every day at 8 am, working until tiffin time. The other old bearer stayed upstairs with Bob, & cooks for him, too.

I made an ironing board, we have an electric iron, small standard lamps, linen, crockery, cutlery, cooking utensils, in fact, we have everything, which is more than most of Jessops' crowd. I almost forgot, we have Ann's small radio too, although at present it is still in Calcutta.

Outside is our garden, looking quite a picture, with a cemented badminton court to keep us fit during the winter evenings. Next month end we get a ten day holiday, so we can at least spend a week away some place. After our return, we have five really good months when we can dance, go to shows & wear decent clothes without melting. Then a few months of hot weather & we are coming home for six months in England. What more could a man want from life?

I often look back at three very rough, tough years in this country, which I used to think were wasted. Our only real fun & interest was work. Lack of transport & places to go made life very dull for us, & I used to long for visits to dances & cinemas & the company of young people. However, all that is gone & life is very pleasant for me now. Of course we have our ups & downs at present in India, with the possibility of anything happening, but that provides the *adventure* that most people get from books.

As for snaps, I haven't been able to get into town recently & Bob hasn't been able to buy any printing papers, but I promise you that as soon as possible I shall send them all, & there are some very good photographs indeed. In fact, Turner Morrisons publish a monthly magazine & the publicity manager has selected two snaps to be printed in the next issue. I am enclosing two pictures of Ann. The small one, where she is coming up the church steps with her boss, Stephens, who gave her away, is just like Ann, smiling & happy. The other one of her alone is not very good. She wasn't feeling too good, but she didn't have black rings under her eyes as this snap shows. (This one was taken at Alipore).

About getting some money from home, Mam, please tell me how to arrange it. Six weeks have elapsed since I wrote to Hutchinson, with never a word in reply. I could surely use that £70 to pay back Mrs. Hoyle.[71] In fact, I promised her repayment when I returned from Gopalpur, but my Calcutta Bank hasn't heard from the Yorkshire Penny Bank. Anyway, my pay goes in after another week &, with a marriage allowance too, I will get straightened out very soon. I was very thankful to Mr. Sitwell, Jessops' Staff, Shalimar Staff, & one or two others who gave us Rs 800 in cash, otherwise I would have been in a mess for ready money.

Best wishes to all the family. I received Arthur's telegram (very nicely worded), & Mrs. Layfield's, but not yours.

Cheerio & love, Fred & *Ann*

Sept. 2nd

Once more, a long interval since my last letter to you, but today, although I was still busy, I had to write because this morning I received a letter from my bank telling me that I had received Rs 665/- or the equivalent of £50. Thanks very, very much, Mam. I really appreciate all you have done for me & hope you did not have too much trouble. I notice that the money was transferred from the Midland Bank, so I guess you had experienced some difficulty in transferring from the Yorkshire Penny direct. Once more, Mam, thanks very much. I am very grateful. The money makes an ideal wedding present.

Talking about wedding presents reminds me that we are still receiving gifts: a set of coffee spoons, a couple of cheques, some stuff on the way from Ohio, u.s.a. We had a letter from America today, telling of the sending of a gift. And of course yours & Aunt Kit's.

Ann is now perfectly fit & looks the picture of health. We are both very glad that she stayed on at Gopalpur for the extra two weeks. Our home is now looking wonderful. Actually I am very proud of her. She has built up a home better than even the Doaks & Howells have got. And food! I have never eaten so well since I left Avonholme. Ann cooks my breakfast herself on her three burner stove. Incidentally, she is up & about at 6 am, while I stay in bed until the 7:30 am buzzer blows. Of course, she usually sleeps in the afternoon after I have gone back to work.

We have the ice-box (Frig.) stacked with cold meats, etc. The small pantry cupboard is full of plum cake, fresh fruit, sweets, biscuits, cocoa, ovaltine, coffee, in fact every little thing to tickle one's appetite. We have drinks ready for when the boys drop in, & a large almirah absolutely bursting with tinned stuff.

On Monday of this week, I was fortunate in being able to arrange for the office station wagon to take Ann into town & pick her up with her stores & bring her back to Dum Dum. Yesterday, Wednesday, she went into town with Mrs. Doak & Mrs. Birchenough in the office car again. They all finished their shopping, sent the parcels back in the car, & went on to have tiffin together.

After tiffin Ann went on to her old office, & to arrange for several dozen more photographs of the wedding. As soon as they are ready I shall send you copies of each.

I left work half an hour early & got a lift into town with Mr. Bury, our acting manager. I met Ann at her mother's place at 5:30 pm & from there we went on to more shopping in the market. Ginger snaps for Mrs. Doak's son Robbie in Darjeeling, lollipops for her daughter Jackie, "Farex" for Mrs. Farren's son Ian. Meanwhile I was buying three-way plugs, tin openers, table mats & what not. We had to find a taxi to take us & all our stuff back to Ann's mother's. Then we went to our usual Chinese cafe for dinner, & on to the Metro Cinema where we saw the film "High Barbaree," not a bad show. Coming out at 11:15 pm, we had a ride back to Dum Dum by taxi.

All this week I have been fixing curtain rods, taps, lights, pulling & pushing furniture around, but finally we have got everything settled & can now start inviting the gang round for dinner.

The weather at present is perfectly lousy, days of gloomy drizzle, with really heavy downpours of rain every couple of hours. Every road is flooded, everything is damp, & it is impossible to go out of doors without getting wet.

Anyway, the Puja (holiday) season is almost here & that will mean the end of the rains & the commencement of the wonderful but short Calcutta winter with dances & parties & plenty of fun. Hope you all keep well, Mam. I have a rough idea that either you or Dad or both of you have birthdays this month. If so, best wishes to you from Ann & myself. Happy times to all the family & Love.

Oct. 11th

The commencement of our annual ten days' holiday, & this year we are not going away anywhere. Our finances are rather short at present due to having to buy so many things for the house. Bob has just returned after two weeks in Darjeeling. He seemed to have had a good time, although it rained a lot during his stay there.

We "foremen" had a rough time in the Works just before the Puja Holidays. You must remember me telling you about the men locking Bill Howell in his office last year & demanding a month's Puja Bonus (which they received). Well, this year the men demanded a bonus again, which the Directors refused. So the men started a go slow policy, which amounted to a sit-down strike in some departments. Also notices were posted all over the place: "We want Bonus", "3 month's Bonus or Go Back London," "Bonus or Die." Even on the foremen's offices, chalked on walls, painted on material & sometimes not very politely written either. Anyway, the Directors called in some high police officials & armed pickets were placed around the Works. They didn't stay long however, as they had to rush off to a jute mill, where the workers had burnt down three large warehouses.

Several large firms had trouble, strikes & lock-outs. But Jessops eventually settled our threatened strike by giving the men a loan of a month's pay, to be repaid in installments. The workers are still very dissatisfied, but the work goes on slowly, very very slowly.

Oct. 26th

You can see by the dates that I started this letter many days ago, put it aside, & just came across it in a drawer. During the holidays, Ann's mother stayed with us for six days & we stayed in town for three days. We filled in the time with swimming, playing snooker at the Club, pictures & shopping. The weather was damp & showery, but now has cleared up. The last few hot days are almost over & already the nights are becoming cool. The usual myriads of mosquitoes & insects appear at night time.

I have had several letters from you recently, *including* the one with the snap of you at Stainton. I remember replying to this one because I mentioned that the weather seemed quite fine for England & the picture seemed like a group of "hens" in America or Australia.

Ann is still as busy as ever, sewing name tags & darning my working shirts. She has knitted me a pair of socks & has almost finished a pullover for me.

We have just bought an electric Singer Sewing Machine, a present from her mother. Our garden, (which is also Ann's department), is looking wizard. We have our regular gardener & another man that I send over from the Works. So far we have put in our cabbages, cauliflowers, beets, carrots, radishes & tomatoes, & sewn all our flower seeds. Incidentally the ground is crawling with ants, so the gardener mixes the seeds with ground rice, or sugar, which they take & leave the seeds. If nothing is mixed, the ants take away the seeds; this sounds surprising, but it is true. Our bananas, which were ripening, were all stolen through the night, but we don't mind. Nobody eats them anyway.

Bob will be off on his home leave in February & I won't be long after him. Arthur Dwyer is now living upstairs in the chummery with him, so he won't be lonely in the top flat.

I read all your news of Violet & Arthur with interest &
look forward to seeing them soon. I am pleased that you
received the snaps & the largest photographs of the
wedding. Ann has told you about getting your gifts. Last
week we received a wonderful lace table cloth from some
of her friends in America, battered in the post, but
unspoilt.

Oct. 27th

This morning I am finishing off this letter in the office.
The daily paper headlines inform us that the Calcutta telephone exchange was burnt down last night, whether acci-
dent or sabotage is not known. This means that the whole
main business area of the city is paralyzed, including
banks, Stock Exchange & Clive Street.

At the Club we are getting ready for the winter season,
organizing dances, tennis parties, & children's parties.
Also snooker & billiard contests, including a mixed
doubles at snooker. During the days when Mrs. Howell
& daughters attended the Club, the men used to drink &
play snooker while the ladies sat & looked at each other.
Anyway, that is all changed now & all the ladies have
learnt to play the game. Every Saturday night the men
must allow the ladies to have the table for one and a half
hours. Old Bill Howell will take a dim view of all this
when he returns. He liked to stay on the table all night.

The men took quite an interest in coaching & although
the girls were a dead loss at first, now Ann, Alice
Birchenough, Joan Farren, Molly Doak, Joan Frost (the
American's wife), Mrs. Kelman are all quite good at the
game. I told you previously that every week the girls have
a couple of hen parties at each other's homes. Now they
all have a morning at the Club playing snooker.

I hope you all keep well at home & at College & at

work away from home. We are quite fit & get plenty of
fun, & I need my fun after all the trouble we put up with
at work these days.

Nov. 26th

Another month & Xmas will be here, & just at present
our weather in India suits an English Xmas. You probably
read of the recent cyclone which hit Bombay & upset the
city with power & communications failures, collapsed
houses & uprooted trees. The backlash of this cyclone
seems to have now reached Calcutta, & we have had a
couple of days of drizzle with a really cold wind. In fact,
although I was wearing a thick pullover this afternoon,
my nose was quite blue. Just imagine the poor old workers, wearing only a thin cotton shirt & cotton dhoti (loin
cloth) & no shoes, how cold the poor devils must have
been.

The men have now drawn their wages, after refusing
for three weeks. The Labour Commissioner who was
dealing with the case went off to Switzerland to an
International Conference & the man who took his place
advised the men to draw their wages, their refusal to do so
having caused much suffering among the poorer paid
men.

Recently the labour have been working better,
although several large engineering companies are on
strike, with no hope of an immediate settlement.

On Wednesday this week I went into town with the
memsahibs on their usual shopping trip. I had a few odds

& ends to buy & also had to have my passport photograph taken. Every Wednesday the girls have the use of
the station wagon for a full day's shopping in town. Mr.
Bury agreed to loan the Works' car every week for this
trip, but everyone seems to think Howell will stop it after
his return.

Ann has been busy making some more curtains today
on her electric sewing machine, while I have been making
hooks & clips & brackets to fix them up over the doors.

Our garden is almost full up now, all the vegetables are
quite high & Ann now fills in her spare time in the garden
showing the mali where to transplant candy tuft,
marigolds, nasturtiums, delphiniums & pinks.

We were pleased to hear that you had seen the film
"The Bishop's Wife." We knew you would enjoy it, so did
we. Another film you shouldn't miss is "Good Sam." We
both thoroughly enjoyed it & it should appeal to you,
too. We go to the cinema regularly twice a week, & see all
the latest releases before they even come to Middlesbro'.

Nov. 29th
Today, Monday, & the weather is still cloudy & cold,
although the rain has ceased. This afternoon I had to take
the station wagon & go to Cossipore, the site of
Calcutta's large Power Station, which is almost
completed. There was a bit of a mix-up with some steelwork we had supplied. I quite enjoyed meeting & talking
with the Site Engineer named Kosis, a Czechoslovakian.
The site engineer of the large fertilizer factory we are
building at Sindri is also a Czech, named Kupa. In our
own Mechanical Works we have a Hungarian engineer
named Vadja, who has only one leg; & now in the
Structural Works we have a Polish draftsman with a name
which nobody can pronounce. He is staying in the shops

for three months to get the hang of things before going to
work in Clive St. office. Also in our head office, we have a
new American draftsman. The present inspector for Merz
& McLellan is a Norwegian named Wefring. I have heard
that the British Govt. are discouraging British Technical
men from coming to India, consequently all the engineering posts are being filled by foreigners.

Dec. 13th

I am really ashamed to be finishing this letter so long
after I started it, but I have just found it in a drawer, & as I
have a few minutes before bedtime, I shall complete the
news.

Recently we have been filling in forms all day & every
day for our Passports, & also for a new scheme of sick &
hospital benefits for Europeans in Calcutta, a sort of
insurance scheme. Then there are the papers we have to
complete to be enrolled as citizens of the United
Kingdom, just as if we were foreigners in a foreign land,
now that India seems to be leaving the Commonwealth.

I have had a rough time getting myself identified as an
Englishman. I have nothing to prove it, all my papers &
passport having been stolen when I first arrived here. I
have asked the High Commissioner for the U.K. to verify
my birth. I gave the birthplace as North Ormesby,
Middlesbrough. I hope this is correct, or I shall have to
become an Indian. You can send me a copy of my birth
certificate, please Mam. Just go to the Registrar, giving
my name & birthday, & he will give you a copy for about
2s-6d.

When I filled in my Passport application form, I had no
documents to prove that I was from England. Feeling
rather doubtful about whether I would get the Public
Notary to sign it, because of the lack of evidence, & not

having an old Passport, I took the morning off work &
went into Calcutta to Orr Dignums Solicitors. The chap I
had to see was named Silverstan, assistant Notary Public.
He opened my application & pursed his lips, asked for my
military papers, which I hadn't got, & then said, "So, you
come from Middlesbro' do you? I was born in Grange
Road."[72]

We talked for an hour about Marton, Nunthorpe,
Ormesby, etc. He used to go around with Betty
Pilkington & he says that his people now live near Sparks'
Cafe or factory or something. Anyway, by a stroke of luck,
the very man whom I was doubtful about convincing
came from my neck of the woods, so my Passport is fixed
up.

On my return to the Works I found a deputation from
the Railway Board Workshops waiting to see me, & just
to add to the list of nationals (foreign) employed in India,
the head man was named Fantom, a Swiss, & another was
named Morgan, a Welshman.

Mr. Duke has now left the Wagon Works to retire in
England & the new manager has taken over, co-inciden-
tally named Howell. I received another of those horrible
Income Tax demand notes informing me that the amount
must be paid within ten days. What a hope. Best wishes to
you all. We got your invitation to the old Pensioners'
Dance this morning.

Dec. 30th

Tomorrow will be the last day of this year & then Saturday will be the first day of the year in which I will be coming home. Only a few months left.

We have had an interesting & busy time this Xmas & the weather has been very seasonable. I left work on Friday the 24th of Dec. at 3 pm so that I could attend the wedding of "Chota" Ford to Maureen Smith, at St. Stephen's Church, Dum Dum. Arthur Dwyer had promised to pick up Ann & myself in his car at 3:45 pm. As usual I was not ready, so Ann went with him. At five minutes to four I managed to complete my dressing & set off from our bungalow, cutting through the jail & climbing over the Church wall at the back.

I arrived to find the service half finished, so stood at the door with Birch, Jock Farren & his little son Ian, & Arthur Dwyer. There seemed to be some hitch in the proceedings because Ann was standing talking to the parson. Eventually she disappeared through the back to return with an arm full of music. Seating herself at the small organ, she began to play, but all sorts of wails & squeaks came forth.

It seems that she had volunteered to play, halfway through the service, & then had to scrounge some music. The organ pedals were faulty & would not spring back. finally an Indian Babu came forward &, squatting on the ground at her feet, worked the pedals by hand. From then, Ann played very well, though unfortunately she couldn't find the music for the wedding march. Anyway having some music brightened up the show a little.

Leaving the church, we all went by car to the Birchenoughs, where we had tea on the lawn. We finished up by "seeing in" Xmas Day, consuming immense quantities of booze & playing the fool in good old Dum Dum style. Ann's mother had arrived at our house during the afternoon to stay over Xmas with us, so after dinner we went back & brought her over to the reception.

Maureen Smith is Alex Smith's youngest girl, the sister of Alice Birchenough. Maureen is not yet sixteen years old, but would pass as twenty in any company. She married a pilot of one of the air companies of Dum Dum, a lad older than me. I have known him since I came to India.

On Xmas day we were swamped with visitors. Birch & Freddy Brennan arrived, both drunk & full of fun. After lunch Bob & Doris came in & we all sang round the piano until Mrs. Frost, Mrs. Farren, & another girl arrived, looking for Birch. We all then went upstairs to Bob's flat for tea (if wanted, whiskey as an alternative).

On the night following (Boxing night), we had a go-as-you-please Fancy Dress Dance. I went as–guess what–a little girl. This was definitely not my idea, but I was outnumbered one to one. Ann certainly made me a smashing dress, crepe paper frills stitched onto a cloth base. Ann went as a Chinese girl. She had a Chinese "Chinchan" or whatever those peculiar long slit-sided dresses are called. Most of the costumes were ridiculous, some very good; but after Egyptians & Sheiks started swapping clothes, the effect was wizard.

One of my mistries from work came up to see me one night (*in his own car*) bringing me three ducks & three hens for Xmas dinners, etc. The hens had some sort of dysentery & eventually three hens & one duck died, so I naturally thought that we would get at least two roast

ducks, but no!!! Ann said she hadn't the heart to kill
them, so we kept them in the garage.

Bob's bearer also bought a duck for Xmas & she
persuaded him not to kill it, so it joined the others in the
run. Then a little later, Bob's bearer bought another hen
& she also wangled that one. On Xmas morning one of
my Mohammedan workmen brought me another hen
which joined the rest of the gang. Now we have two
drakes & a duck, & two hens. All the female fowls are
laying, & they are so tame that they wander around
behind Ann like dogs. So no more roast chicken & duck
for me from now on.

Jan. 4th

At last we have started the New Year, after a succession
of parties & outings. On New Year's Eve Ann & I went
into town, had dinner out &, after meeting a crowd of her
old office friends, went to the 9pm show at the
Lighthouse Cinema. The picture showing was Bing
Crosby in the Emperor Waltz, a really smashing entertainment; don't miss it!

Coming out of the cinema we wandered down
Chowringhee looking for a place to dance. Eventually we
got into a packed Firpo's, where we wrestled on the
crowded dance floor & finally were swamped by the
howling throng as midnight came along.

We left Firpo's at 1 am & then drifted round to *somebody's* house draped in balloons & streamers (us, not the
house). Also, on Jan. 2nd we went to a cocktail party in
Dum Dum, held at the home of Bill Frost, the American
lad, & his wife. We had a really hectic time there.

Now I shall have to take this opportunity of wishing all
the far-flung Turnbull family a Happy & Prosperous New
Year, & let's hope it is a Peaceful one too.

I have been given a lecture by Ann because I didn't send you a Xmas present. She was very mad about it, so please let me know your birthday. She says that I am the most thoughtless person she has ever met.

I have now received my passport & am all set for coming home in July. The Labour in the Works are still causing trouble because they didn't get a bonus, & are going slow & attempting sit down strikes. However, I am fit & well, & still enjoy life.

Best wishes to you all. Keep smiling.

    Love,
    Fred & Ann

1949

Jan. 13th

Dear Mam,

Thanks very much for sending my birth certificate. I got it yesterday with the letter enclosed. Ann also has just had her passport renewed & as I have received my new passport, we were able to have our British Citizenship papers signed & attested by George Clark of the Gramophone Company, who is an attestation officer.

Last night we walked through the sugar cane fields up to the Gramophone Company to meet George Clark. It was a lovely moonlit night, the jackals howling in the jungle, & a cool breeze was blowing, so walking kept us comfortably warm.

On Jan. 11th, Bill Howell arrived by plane at 4:30 pm. I didn't see him until yesterday afternoon in the Works. He looks very fit & seems to have put on weight, although he says that he didn't like England. I understand that he will start work on Monday.

Today is a Muslim festival & so we have a holiday. Ann's mother came up from town yesterday evening to stay today with us. We are just having a quiet day in the bungalow.

Sunday the 16th

Today we came back from Calcutta by taxi with Bob &
Doris. We always go into town on Saturdays & Ann & I
stay overnight at her mother's place. We had dinner out,
& went to the cinema to see "The Bride Goes Wild" at the
Metro, a picture you would enjoy, especially the kids at
the end.

This morning we went off to the Club for the usual
tennis & snooker (it is still too cold for swimming). Bill
Howell was there, grumbling as usual about the cold &
the buses in England. He doesn't deserve a holiday.

Also at the Club was a fellow named Broughton, who
books the passages for the Anchor Line. After a talk with
him this morning he says that he will try to get our
passages fixed up for the end of June on the "Caledonia,"
which suits me fine.

Jan. 21st

I just don't seem able to find time to write letters. I
suppose it is because I have my hands full at work, & my
spare time is absolutely filled with odd jobs.

I can't remember whether I told you about the party
we had at our bungalow on Jan. 7th. All the Dum Dum
Jessops crowd were there, as well as Bill Frost & his wife
(the Americans). We cleared our large front room for
dancing to Bob's radiogram, lit up the badminton court,
& Ann scrounged some Scotch whiskey from her stores in
town. We had a big sit down meal in our dining room
with fifteen people at dinner. The gang thoroughly
enjoyed it, & as Birch's birthday coincided, and also the
Doaks' wedding anniversary, we just couldn't get them to
go home.

Now for the Dum Dum news: Joan Farren has just
come out of a Nursing Home where she had an operation

for appendicitis. The Howell mem & miss-sahibs are scheduled to arrive at the end of the month. The Doaks leave for England next month, & as they are selling all their furniture, etc., they are not expected to return to India. Mr. Duke, the manager of Wagon Works, has packed in & left for home, his place having been filled by another Mr. Howell, who was recruited from Lahore. Bob Kraus leaves for home at the end of February. The Birchenoughs are going in June. Everyone is looking forward to their home leave because conditions in the Works are going from bad to worse. The Labour is just ruling the roost now.

You have probably read in the papers of the trouble in Calcutta, curfews in most districts from 5:30 pm, military & police are patrolling the affected areas, while mobs of hooligans are throwing bombs & stones, setting fire to tramcars & buses, & are being dispersed by police with tear gas, lathi charges, &, in many cases, by rifle fire. About twenty trams have been gutted by fire so far. The riots were started on Tuesday, when students set off in a procession to see Pandit Nehru, who was in Calcutta. The police broke up the procession with rifle fire. Five people were killed & about 50 injured.

The next day there were processions protesting against the police firing. They were joined by thousands of refugees from East Bengal (Pakistan), who are all complaining about having to leave their homes. Other gangs were protesting against aggression in Indonesia, while tramway employees who are very dissatisfied with their pay these days, were setting fire to every vehicle they could lay hands on. Also, Calcutta has thousands of "goondahs", that is, killers who were left over from the Political riots, who just take advantage of such a situation to loot, burn & pillage.

I am afraid that India is getting into a state which will soon become like Burma & China, because Communists are very active & they naturally thrive under conditions of poverty, labour unrest, & general indiscipline. Everybody is underfed, the wages are high, but insufficient, & most of India's working classes are ripe to start any sort of trouble. Meanwhile, with all this trouble on his own doorstep, Pandit Nehru is discussing the problem of *Indonesia*.

Yesterday I received a rather nice letter from Mrs. Layfield, telling me of what had happened to some of my old schoolmates.

Yesterday, Ann had a tooth extracted, under gas. We went into Calcutta on Wednesday & stayed the night, calling in at the Dentists at 8 am the next morning.

The weather is getting slightly warmer, although the nights are still cold. In February, Ann has a birthday on the 4th, the Sandeman dance is on the 5th, the Lodge Installation Banquet is about the 15th, & the Jardine Golf Competition, to be held at the Royal Golf Club, is on the 20th. I have put my name down to play, but will have to borrow some clubs from somewhere. Today I received a letter from you, & note that Violet is back at College, & that Dad still goes to his innumerable committee meetings. Best wishes to all the family.

[Enclosed: an article on the Calcutta riots, headlined, "5 Killed And 57 Hurt Yesterday"]

Jan. 30th

Dear Mam,

Sunday, & one year since Mahatma Gandhi was assassinated, although the ideals for which he strived during the latter part of his life aren't very conspicuous in present-day India.

This month is a very lively time for me, with several interesting events. Last week was the anniversary of our engagement. As it fell on a weekday, we had a quiet day at home, but decided to celebrate at the end of the week. Therefore yesterday (Sat.) we went into Calcutta, taking our dress togs with us. Ann was dropped into town by Howell, who was going to Howrah Station to pick up his wife & daughters who were expected to arrive at tiffin time. Bob & I followed after work in the foremen's bus.

I arrived at Ann's mother's & had my lunch & then had a sleep until Ann came back from shopping. Then we lashed up in our evening clothes. Ann has changed her wedding dress into an evening dress & wore that outfit. The nights are still cold, so we can wear warm clothes comfortably.

We took a taxi to Firpo's, where we got a table for two right alongside the dance floor. I didn't have time to eat very much dinner, because Ann dragged me up for all the dances. The Doaks & Arthur Dwyer were also there, they went on to a dance at the Swimming Club. We left at 9 pm & went round to the New Empire to see the C.A.T.S. revue. The Calcutta Amateur Theatrical Society provided the show from local talent, with topical gags, good

singing, dances, sketches & some good music from five
pianos. It was a thoroughly enjoyable evening & quite a
change from our usual visit to the cinema.

We visited the Club this morning & met the Howells,
& Matt Ewing, who arrived by air yesterday. What a
difference six months in the British Isles makes to them
all. They all looked wonderfully fit. Mrs. Howell especially looked ten years younger, & she was very tastefully
dressed too.

This week on Feb. 4th Ann has a birthday, so I will
have to drop into town to pick up her present. Please give
my best wishes to Arthur & Violet for their birthdays on
the 9th & 11th, for their future happiness & success.
As far as I know, we will be sailing on the *Caledonia*
about the 5th of July, & already we have stacks of places to
visit. The Doaks want us to visit them in Cardiff &
Glasgow; we are going to meet the "Birches" in Crewe,
Ann's relatives in Bristol, Bournemouth & London, &
then, of course, my own thousands of relations.

I am really looking forward to my six months & once
more to see the green fields, & the moors of England.
Everyone is disappointed by the British people they meet,
especially the younger generation in England, who seem
to have forgotten how to enjoy themselves as we used to
do, with our camping, cycling & tomfoolery. They say
that the pubs are full of young lads & the dance halls are
packed with hoardes of young, painted, 14 year old girls,
anxious to have a good time.

You asked about the dogs in your last letter. Our
Meggy is still as full of fun & intelligence as ever, while
Bob's black cocker, Mike, has grown into a curly black
bear & just bursts with mischief & devilry. He has grown
into a really comical looking hound. He has a rather
remarkable history, for some time ago he went off into a

fit &, after tearing madly around the upstairs rooms, he
jumped over the verandah rails & fell 25 feet into a
concrete drain. Bob's bearer took him into the nearest
veterinarian college in a rickshaw, where he was detained
as a suspected rabid dog. However, he is now fit & lively
as ever.

The trouble has died down in Calcutta, although there
is still a lot of unrest, & I am afraid that sooner or later
there will be industrial chaos here, unless some settlement
is made about decreasing production & increasing wages
& cost of living at present happening in India. We are
having plenty of trouble in Jessop & Co. at present &
discipline is practically non-existent. Bill Howell never
walks into the shops these days, but spends his time working out a scheme of production bonus. We the foremen all
agree with him, because, under present conditions, a man
cannot be discharged or suspended; consequently the
men know that if they don't do any work, no action can
be taken, & they still draw their wages. Therefore, there
must be some incentive, where, if a man works hard, he
will get more money. That is why Bill Howell is trying to
start some scheme of bonus on monthly output.

Matt Ewing has come to Structural Works to take over
from Bob for six months, & another fellow, name of
Reid, is coming out to take my place.

Feb. 5th

Yesterday was Ann's birthday. We went to town in the
morning as Ann unfortunately had to see a doctor & have
an X-ray taken. She has (suspected) appendicitis. After
leaving the doctor's we went round to Calcutta's largest
store, where there was a sale. I bought her an American
dress for 50 chips, one-third of the original price. She
intends to wear it for Jessops' Golf Tournament, when all

the mem sahibs compete with each other for the title of
Bird of Paradise.

Tonight we are going to the Masons' Dance at
Cossipore Club. All the Dum Dum gang are going,
including the Howells. Incidentally, we now have
another Howell in Jessop & Co. He has taken over the
managership of Wagon Works & Mechanical.

I almost forgot, I bought Ann a silver brush & comb
for her birthday. She says it is important that I should
mention it to you .

Best wishes to you all & love

Fred

[The last letter Fred wrote was to Ernie & Ethel Cooper.]

c/o Jessop & Co.
Dum Dum
24 Parganas
W. Bengal
Feb. 16th

Dear Ernie & Ethel

I have received your air letter in which you paint a dark &
gloomy picture of England. However, these days it doesn't
create any optimism if one looks to the future, therefore it
is better to live in the present & enjoy life as much as
possible. You have probably deduced by now that China
"HAS HAD IT" & that Burma "IS HAVING IT," & from

the trend of events here in the past few months, India "WILL HAVE IT." The Indian Govt. has now decided that abandonment of food & cloth controls was ill-advised & they (the Govt.) intend to re-introduce rationing & controls of everything possible. Meanwhile, food stocks are very low, inflation is with us, & every worker in India is dissatisfied & is making plans for going on strike.

The workers in my firm of Jessop & Co. have been going slow for a year now, & discipline is so low that I don't know whether I shall return to the worry & responsibility here. Life is too short to spend in a constant state of mental stress. Unfortunately, I have a nice home & compound here, & the next contract offered to me by the firm is decidedly attractive, in fact. I could really save money & live well on the salary proposed. However, I have another four months ahead of me before I sail on the *Caledonia* at the end of June, & many things can happen between now & then.

Last Sunday "the wife" & I went to the Royal Golf Club in Calcutta, where our firm was running their annual Golf Competition. I went round the course in 130 strokes, which is fairly ghastly. Less my handicap of 36 gave me a score of 94, which was the worst in the competition. However, even if I didn't know a driver from an iron, I had a good time. We finished up with the usual tiffin & the usual drunken sahibs being dragged away by their angry memsahibs.

The cold weather is almost ended and the days are warm & clear. In fact, February is the nicest month in Bengal apart from mosquitoes.

Today being Wednesday, all the Dum Dum mem-sahibs take the Company's station wagon & sally forth into town to do their shopping & attempt to reduce the bank balances of their husbands to shreds. My wife has joined in the fray & so I am a bachelor for today. (I shall forgive her if she brings home a bottle of Scotch as she usually does).

My manager, Howell, complains bitterly of his teeth, but don't get bothered, Ernie. Nobody has *ever* succeeded in pleasing Howell.[73]

Today was a momentous occasion in our compound. My wife, being very soft-hearted, cannot stand the thought of killing chickens, etc. for meals. At Xmas time several of my men made us presents of fowls & ducks for the table, but Ann kept them all as pets in one of our old garages. We have two drakes & a duck, a cock & a hen. The hen decided to go broody, so we let her sit on seven eggs. This morning we found that four little chicks have hatched out, & Ann is absolutely thrilled with the "ruddy" things.

Our garden looks wonderful, all our flowers are in bloom & we have a job keeping the little Indian kids from stealing them for their Puja in the temples. We are living on our own beets, cabbages, cauliflowers, peas, carrots, turnips, onions & tomatoes these days.

Most of our recreational time is spent at our Club in Dum Dum, with either tennis or swimming on Sundays, & snooker & billiards through the week. Also, every Saturday we go into town for a visit to the cinema, with dinner & dancing at one of the large hotels.

I still follow the English Football reports with interest, & think that Manchester Utd. will win the F.A. Cup, & that Middlesbrough will slide down into the second Division, even with the help of Mannion & Hardwick. The rest of the team seem to be a gang of cripples. I was pleased to hear, too, of your Boys' Club team's successes. You seem to be doing a useful job for the youth of Ormesby.

Several weeks ago the Victoria Memorial on the Calcutta Maidan was opened for the public for the first time since the war. It is a huge white building of superb

architecture, commemorating Queen Victoria, who by
the way, is the only British ruler that the Indians seem to
have respected. The building houses several of her
personal belongings: piano, writing desk, etc., with
letters written by her. The whole place is a record of the
British in India from the time of Robert Clive.

I was struck by reports in old documents that those old
adventurers were really a gang of brave (not heroes, but)
rogues, who built up the British Empire more by daring
& swashbuckling than by any true sense of loyalty to the
Crown. A different story from that given in my old school
history books. However, that phase of British History has
ended, & the British Govt.'s present policy seems to be to
get rid of our far distant lands as quickly as possible.
Whether this will prove beneficial to all concerned
remains to be seen.

What happened to all the old scout patrol, Ernie?
Derek Vincent, Tommy Brighton, Jack Evans, Norman
Miller & Harry Benson–do they all still live in Ormesby's
sylvan glades, or have they gone abroad?

By the way, in my last letter I asked if you could give
me any dope on British Income Tax. I have received two
demands for the payment of £57 to H.M. the King,
supposed to be outstanding from the year 1943/44. As I
paid my usual "Pay as you earn," & left England understanding that I was clear, can you give me any idea what
this is for? I have about £160 in Post War Credits due to
me. Are these payable now, or could they be accepted in
lieu of my debt? Because of the difficulties of correspondence, I have made no attempt to question the Income
Tax people.

I hope that you & your wife & Beryl are well & happy;
our best wishes to you both. See you soon

Fred & Ann

A̲MONG FOUR BRITISH EMPLOYEES
of a Calcutta engineering works murdered on Saturday
by members of the Indian Revolutionary Communist
Party , was Frederick Gower Turnbull (28), of Middlesbrough.

The bodies of Turnbull, and Arthur Dwyer (37), of
Halifax, (earlier reported of Middlesbrough), and
Frederick Charles Brennan, an Anglo-Indian, were
recovered from two pressure furnaces.

Altogether four British or Anglo-Indian employees
were killed by terrorists in Saturday night's raid on the
works of Jessop and Company.

The fourth man, Felix Augier (42), died in hospital
from stab wounds.

Matthew Ewing, a British foreman at Jessops, was
struck on the head. He was rescued by loyal workers,
who dragged him to safety over a wall.

There has been considerable labour unrest at the
works, due to a reduction of over 150 workers recently.
The raiders' savage tactics suggest that they aimed to
stiffen malcontents in opposition to the Indian Government's gradually succeeding efforts to break the general
strike threat.

Indian and Pakistani police are combing the country to round up stray batches of raiders.

Some escaped by boat and others in cars and lorries. Fifteen rifles and several hand grenades were captured by the police. ...

Middlesbrough Evening Gazette, February 28, 1949

NOTES

Note: Where particular Hindi or Anglo-Indian words or phrases are not defined, it is usually because Fred himself explains them in a later letter.

1. In wartime England baths were strictly limited to 4 inches of water, so this was a special luxury.

2. Imperial Chemical Industries, where Violet worked, was considered an elite place to work, hence the dig.

3. The family said goodbye to Fred, thinking he was going to London, and not knowing where he was to sail from. There was a wartime ban on information about the arrivals and departures of all trains, planes and ships (and all road signs were removed as well); so it was unexpected to hear from him in Scotland.

4. Ernie Cooper, a friend from the village, who was in the home guard.

5. Housey Housey is Bingo.

6. The Brains Trust was a radio programme, which included Julian Huxley, Professor Joad, etc.

7. Sixpence

8. Two shillings

9. Four shillings

10. The number has been cut out by the censors.

11. Short for Entertainments National Service Association, they entertained the troops.

12. The village home guard.

13. Cross Keys was the pub in Guisborough at the foot of the moors. It was Fred's favourite drinking spot, as well as everyone else's.

14. Corporation Rd. is one of the main streets of Middlesbrough, so the monsoon smelled like an English industrial city in winter to Fred.

15. Tips or gratuities.

16. Chung king, or more properly Chong qing, was the capital of China from 1937 to 1946.

17. "Fred was more interested in sports than in dances," Violet explains, "but just before he left for India, he decided he'd better learn some social graces. So I taught him to waltz & to foxtrot, but we would always end up collapsed with laughter, because he was fine in a straight line, but had trouble navigating corners. His dancing obviously improved a great deal while he was in India."

18. A portable turntable.

19. pucca = proper, jungli = of the jungle, walla = a person.

20. One shilling and sixpence.

21. Tiffin is an Anglo-Indian word for a light meal such as lunch or tea.

22.. Two local village boys, probably with the Army.

23. A mistri is one who works with his hands, such as a carpenter or a mechanic.

24. Fred is describing the Whitby Abby route to the River Tees, called Donkey Lane, an ancient road on which they lived.

25. Violet worked with Harry Mallaby in the office at I.C.I.

NOTES   263

26. The Illustrated London News

27. Adam's Ale is water.

28. Harry Mallaby.

29. The Vincents, friends from Ormesby, made Fred godfather to their new baby, Diana.

30. Violet eventually received the shoes, beautiful handmade goat-skin ones.

31. "At this time I'd written to Fred about the popularity of Russia in England, because they had made a great sweep through Europe, freeing several countries. He always teased me about my leftist leanings, which had their start with the Spanish Civil War, of course." (Violet)

32. Jai Hind means "Victory for India." The customary response is Bande Mataram, which means "I bow to my motherland."

33. Fourteen shillings.

34. The teacher of the village school. She taught all the children of Ormesby, ages five to fourteen, all in one room, and was greatly respected by all the kids. Fred was always a great favourite of hers.

35. Goondah is a Hindi word for thug, one who steals and bullies his way through life, and takes advantage of times of upheaval.

36. Cargo Fleet Iron Co. Ltd. of Middlesbrough was where Fred's father worked, and where Fred & Bob apprenticed.

37. For every 12 million G.N.P. produced in India, 11 million was taken out.

38. The snakeskin bag never came, nor did many other things he sent to the family.

39. B.U. stood for bread units, ration coupons designated for bread. It seemed peculiar to be rationed for bread yet, so long after the war ended.

40. A tamasha is a show or programme, often put on as part of a celebration.

41. The Jemadar is the janitor responsible for the toilets.

42. In Scottish tradition, the first person to enter a house on New Year's Day (the first-foot) should, for luck, be a dark-haired male bearing gifts of food, drink & fuel.

43. The Littlewoods coupon refers to the English football pool, which Fred continued to bet on. Scrubbed meant cancelled.

44. Robert Clive (1725-74), a British soldier who became an administrator of the East India Co., Clive eventually became sole ruler, in all but name, of Bengal. He reformed the civil service in India along military lines.

45. Topee is the Hindi word for the pith helmets Europeans wore for protection against the sun.

46. A sort of Yorkshire folk song about being lost on the moors without a hat. Ilkley Moor is a place near Leeds, and b'aht t'at is dialect for without a hat.

47. Coir is a coconut fibre, used to make rope, mats and coarse brushes.

48. Jack Simpson.

49. The Perrys were related to Mrs. Howell.

50. Mr. Daggett was the herdsman for the Huddlestones in Ormesby. He had a large family, all of whom went to the village school with Fred, Violet and Arthur.

51. Middlesbrough cinemas.

52. A stick, usually made of bamboo and bound or tipped with metal.

53. An outspoken advocate of Indian independence, Bose was at various times President of the All India Trades Union and President of the Indian National Congress.

54. A specific area of a village, often the poorer area.

55. Storeroom.

56. Gate-keeper.

57. A stick or club with a blade on the end.

58. Uncle Tom Cobley & all is a phrase from a popular English song and means the same as "everybody & his brother."

59. A romantic duet from the music halls.

60. In reality, Arthur was quite thin.

61. Satyagraha means "a vow to maintain the truth." It was basic to Gandhi's doctrine of passive resistance, and was meant to be used with ahimsa, or non-violence.

62. Models of the tombs of Husein and Hasan, brothers who were Shi'ite spiritual leaders (imams) from the seventh century.

63. Redcar is about 45 minutes by bus from Ormesby.

64. The theme song for an English radio programme.

65. It was not until September of 1948 that Hyerabad surrendered to Indian forces and agreed to join the Indian Union.

66. Char is four; chota is small; peg is whiskey; and lao is bring, in Hindi.

67. Crore means ten million rupees.

68. A reference to the A & B menus at Firpo's.

69. Chae is tea.

70. The Royal Calcutta Golf Club. Popsies meant pretty, young girls.

71. Ann's mother.

72. Grange Road is the main street of Middlesbrough.

73. Ernie Cooper was a dentist.

ISBN 0-921227-04-3

Most of the photographs Fred sent home were taken and printed by Bob Kraus.

CANADIAN CATALOGUING IN PUBLICATION DATA

Turnbull, Frederick Gower, 1920-1949
    Remember me to everybody

ISBN 0-921227-04-3

1. Turnbull, Frederick Gower, 1920-1949 –
Correspondence. 2. India – History – 20th
century. 3. India – Politics and government –
1919-1947. 4. India – Politics and government –
1947-   . I. Rule, Bernadette, 1951-   .
II. Title.

DS481.T87A4 1996   954.03´59´092   C96-932456-1

This book was designed by Jaggard Blount and was typeset and printed at Coach House Printing, Toronto, in November 1996. There was a second printing in December 1997. The typefaces are Hiroshige and Galliard and the wood engraving is by Wesley W. Bates.